KNITTED SHAWLS,
STOLES, & SCARVES

NANCIE M. WISEMAN

Martingale
& COMPANY

Martingale & Company
20205 144th Avenue NE
Woodinville, WA 98072-8478
www.martingale-pub.com

Printed in China
05 04 03   8 7 6 5 4

Library of Congress Cataloging-in-Publication Data
Wiseman, Nancie M.
    Knitted shawls, stoles, and scarves / Nancie M. Wiseman.
        p. cm.
    ISBN 1-56477-331-0
    1. Shawls. 2. Stoles (Clothing). 3. Scarves.
    4. Knitting—Patterns. I. Title.

TT825 . W58 2001
746.43'20432—dc21   00-056839

CREDITS

PRESIDENT • Nancy J. Martin
CEO • Daniel J. Martin
PUBLISHER • Jane Hamada
EDITORIAL DIRECTOR • Mary V. Green
EDITORIAL PROJECT MANAGER • Tina Cook
TECHNICAL EDITOR • Ursula Reikes
COPY EDITOR • Karen Koll
DESIGN AND PRODUCTION MANAGER • Stan Green
ILLUSTRATOR • Robin Strobel
COVER DESIGNER • Stan Green
TEXT DESIGNER • Trina Stahl
DETAIL PHOTOGRAPHY • Brent Kane
FASHION PHOTOGRAPHY • Anna Midori Abe
HAIR AND MAKEUP • Shannon Rasheed
FASHION STYLIST • Emilie Maslow

ACKNOWLEDGEMENTS

MY GRATITUDE AND THANKS TO:
Marlene Fong of Sacramento, California, and Kay Holt of Freeport, Texas, for knitting five of the projects in this book using only scribbled notes and drawings. And to my husband, William Attwater, for cooking, running errands, and canceling your vacation in Hawaii. I will always love you and hope you know you are in my heart whenever I am away from you.

CONTENTS

INTRODUCTION

As we can see from looking back at old fashion magazines, shawls, stoles, and scarves have been around for a very long time. From shawls that Grandma would have worn to those in the shapes, colors, and textures of today, shawls, stoles, and scarves are still a mainstay of the working and everyday wardrobe.

Who doesn't love to wrap up in a warm, cozy shawl? Wonderful to wear, shawls not only make you feel elegant, but they look elegant too. They are also a wonderful way to use some of the more glamorous yarns available today.

Many beginning knitters choose a scarf as a first project and then find it too boring to complete. How many of you started a scarf as your first knitting project and never finished it because it seemed to go on forever? When I started designing shawls and scarves with shaping and texture, I found that they were more fun to knit and wear. They were more fun to wear because they fit better, no longer the straight, garter-stitch length of knitting that bunched up at the back of neck. They were more fun to knit because they used interesting, fun patterns.

Whether you are a new knitter or a knitter who has been knitting "all your life," you will find that the chapters in this book will help you with design and technique questions. Each project will inspire and teach a new technique or new idea in the creation of shape or texture. Not just a pattern book, this book can be used as a guide or reference to further your knitting knowledge.

Some of the techniques used in designing the shawls can be a bit challenging to learn on a garment that has to "fit." Gauge, that all-important set of numbers, becomes less of a burden when you knit shawls and scarves. Although it is still important, gauge should not be a cause for worry when you start a project using a new technique. These projects will make learning a new technique fun, and you won't have to knit a whole fitted garment to learn it. It isn't often that we can show our knitting expertise on a garment so simply shaped.

One of the most exciting things for me in writing this book was creating a design and then finding the perfect yarn to show it off. There is no shortage of wonderful yarns on the market today, and I love all of them. The challenge was choosing the yarn that would best show the style and pattern of the shawl or scarf and would also make it comfortable to wear. I wanted to give you, the knitter, lots of options in regard to needle size and the weight and fiber content of the yarns used.

HISTORICALLY SPEAKING

THE SHAWL HAS been significant in the fashion world for hundreds of years. The word "shawl" is of Persian origin. Some of the first shawls seen in the mid-eighteenth century in England were imported from Persia, India, and Kashmir by the British. They were probably purchased because of their color and beauty and sent home to England as gifts to loved ones. These embroidered or printed textiles were also worn and loved by Queen Victoria in the mid-1800s.

The Shetland Islands, located in the North Sea above Scotland, are renowned for their knitted shawls and scarves. The shape, style, and design of Shetland shawls and woven Indian shawls are remarkably similar. Many of the woven patterns in the Indian shawls were duplicated in the knitted lace made by the women of the Shetland Islands. The famous lacework in these shawls is a tribute to the Shetland women, who often created the amazing gossamer webs without pattern books or instructions.

Shawls and scarves throughout fashion history have been made in many variations, including cover-ups, tippets, mantles, fascinators, and Nubians. A tippet is a covering for the neck and shoulders, usually of fur or wool, with long ends that hang down the front. A mantle is a kind of cape. The fascinator, popular in the early 1900s, was a head scarf with ends that rested on the wearer's shoulders. In her book *No Idle Hands*, Anne L. Macdonald reports that "a 'Nubian' was usually described as a fleecy woolen scarf about three yards long and about a half yard wide, or sometimes as a triangular shawl."[1]

Stoles have been known as sontags or shoulder wraps, and scarves worn around the neck were and are still known as mufflers and ascots.

When knitting shawls was the thing to do in the mid-1800s, books, magazines, and newspapers began to publish patterns for them. There were, however, very few pictures, and so the written description had to convey what the item would be like when finished. Still, the directions and descriptions fell short of what we are used to seeing today. The directions for a Shetland Island shawl might say how many stitches to cast on, suggest a lace pattern to use, and end with a tip on embellishment; for example, "A scarlet or violet crocheted border improves it."[2] I suppose such brief instructions were better than nothing at all.

Any fabric could eventually work its way into a shawl, stole, or scarf. For the pioneer woman, the chosen fabric was probably dark so it wouldn't need a lot of washing, and it may have been scratchy, homespun material. But today we have the luxury of knitting with wonderful natural and synthetic fibers. This makes shawls, stoles, and scarves the perfect palette for learning new techniques and experimenting with yarns and fibers.

1. Anne L. Macdonald, *No Idle Hands: The Social History of American Knitting* (New York: Ballantine Books, 1988), 58.

2 *Ibid.*, 156, quoting Elvina Corbould, *The Lady's Knitting Book* (New York: Anson D. F. Randolph and Co., 1879), 34.

TECHNIQUES AND TERMINOLOGY

CHARTS

CHARTS ARE A good way of writing knitting patterns and are easy to use once you get used to them. They allow you to see a picture of what the actual knitting will look like when completed. Symbols can vary from pattern writer to pattern writer, but for the most part they tend to be consistent. It really doesn't matter what symbol is used for the decrease "knit 2 together" as long as the directions tell you what the symbols mean.

Here are the basic rules for chart reading:

- Knit rows are usually the odd-numbered rows and may have the numbers listed on the right side of the chart. Read the chart from right to left for knit rows.

- Purl rows are read from left to right and are usually the even-numbered rows, with the numbers listed on the left side of the chart.

- On lace charts the wrong side row is often not charted because it is often a plain knit or purl row. The directions should tell you what you are supposed to do on the wrong side rows if they aren't charted.

- Each square on a chart represents a stitch. There are times in lace charting when a blank section might be placed in the chart so the flow of the pattern may be seen more easily.

- Coloring the sections in intarsia charts will make them easier to read after they have been enlarged. Sometimes the symbols used to designate colors are very similar and difficult to read. Such symbols can make it easy to choose the wrong color.

- Use a ruler or straightedge to help you keep track of rows. Stick-on notes work well too. Place the ruler or marker above where you are working, not below. You can then see what has already been knit and compare it to the chart as you work. This will eliminate a lot of counting.

- Mark off each row as you work. Use a pencil so you can erase the marks if you have to rework a row. You can use a highlighter pen, but if you have to rip out a section you will be reknitting sections that are already marked off, and it might be confusing.

CABLE CAST ON

USE THE CABLE cast on for all cast-on stitches worked with knitting already in progress, as in the Textured Squares Mohair Shawl and the Textured Squares Scarf. Insert right knitting needle between two stitches on left needle. Knit a stitch but do not drop any stitches off left needle. Place the new stitch back on the left needle, inserting the left needle into the stitch from the right side, or by your right thumb. Repeat as many times as stitches are needed.

PROVISIONAL CAST ON

USING A SIZE G or H crochet hook and waste cotton yarn in a color that contrasts with your project yarn, crochet a loose chain, 1 chain for each number of stitches needed for cast on, plus 5 or 6 extra stitches. Cut yarn, leaving about a 6" tail. Finish off so that the chain will not unravel. Tie a knot in the tail. Using the working yarn and the appropriate needle, turn the chain to the wrong side and pick up a stitch into the loop on the back of the chain. You can skip chains if necessary. You will remove this waste yarn later. Pick up the correct number of stitches for the pattern (this is a right side row), and then continue with the directions.

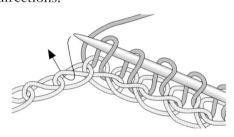

When you are ready to remove the crochet chain, start at the end with the knot you created when you finished the chain and gently "unzip" the chain. As you remove the chain, place the loops of the main yarn on a knitting needle to be worked later. The crochet chain will "unzip" from one end only. Placing the knot in the tail tells you at what end to start.

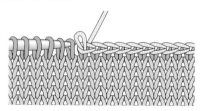

I CORD

DID YOU KNOW "I cord" stands for "idiot cord"? Cast on 3 stitches to a double-pointed needle. *Do not turn.* Knit across, pulling the yarn tightly across the back. Slide the stitches to the opposite end of the needle.* Repeat from * to * for desired length. Bind off.

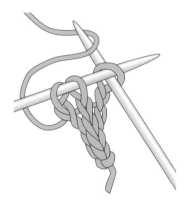

SLIP STITCHES

Slip 1 stitch (Sl 1): Insert the right knitting needle into the stitch as if to purl. Move the stitch to the right needle. Do not move the yarn to the purl position before you slip the stitch. This keeps the stitch in the correct position for when it is eventually knitted or purled.

When working slip stitches, it is important to keep the yarn on the side that does not create floating yarn across the right side of the knitting, unless directed to do so. The following terms are meant to tell you where the yarn should be located before a stitch is slipped. They refer to the direction of your knitting, not the right and wrong side of your knitting. "In front" means toward you, not the right side of the work, and "in back" means away from you, not the wrong side of the work. These terms are often thought to be understood and not even put into the directions.

- With Yarn in Back (wyib): Move or leave the yarn to the back of the work.

- With Yarn in Front (wyif): Move or leave the yarn to the front of the work.

Knit 1 below: Knit into the center of the stitch that lies directly below the first stitch on the left needle and wrap the yarn in the usual manner. Pull the new stitch through and drop the stitch off the left needle as you normally would.

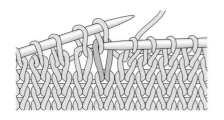

INCREASES

Traditional increase (inc): Knit in the front and back of a stitch. Knit the stitch as you normally would, but do not drop the stitch off the left needle. Move the right knitting needle toward the back of the work and knit into the back of the stitch. Drop the stitch off the left needle. This creates 2 stitches out of 1.

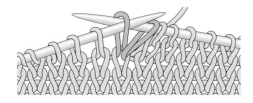

Make 1 increase (M1): This is a more invisible increase than the traditional increase, but it can be worked only between 2 stitches. Insert the right knitting needle under the yarn, from front to back, that connects the stitch just worked and the stitch on the left needle. Place the loop on the left needle. Knit into the back of the loop. This twists the stitch so there is no hole in the knitting. If there is a hole, the stitch was knitted incorrectly.

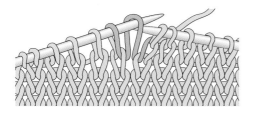

DECREASES

Knit 2 together (K2tog): Insert the right knitting needle into 2 stitches on the left needle and knit the 2 together. This is a basic decrease that slants toward the right.

Slip, slip, knit (SSK): Slip 1 stitch on the left needle as if to knit. Slip the next stitch on the left needle as if to knit. Insert the left knitting needle into the front of the 2 stitches from left to right. Wrap the yarn around the right needle and knit the 2 stitches together. Another basic decrease, but this one slants toward the left.

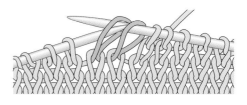

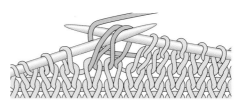

Slip, slip, slip, knit (SSSK): Worked the same as SSK using 3 stitches. Slip 1 stitch as if to knit. Slip a second stitch as if to knit. Slip a third stitch as if to knit. Insert the left needle into the front of the 3 stitches and knit the 3 together.

Central chain decrease (CC Dec): Slip the next 2 stitches together as if to knit. Knit 1. Pass the 2 slipped stitches over together (p2sso).

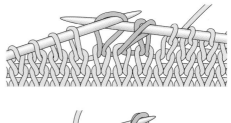

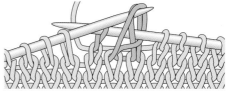

Basic Short Rows

THE ABBREVIATION FOR the method used for creating short rows is "W and T" for "wrap and turn."

On the knit side of the work: Knit to the designated stitch. Slip the next stitch from the left needle to the right needle as if to purl. Move the yarn between the needles to the front and slip the stitch back to the left needle. Be sure the yarn is down and out of your way. Move the yarn to the back. Don't pull the yarn too tightly.

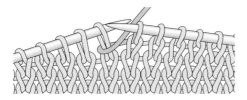

Move yarn to back of work.

Turn your work and purl back across the stitches that were previously knit. Continue in this manner until all short rows are worked. It will look like there is yarn wrapped around a stitch in a manner that resembles a purl bar. There will also be a small gap between the stitches on the needle where the turn was made. On subsequent rows the "wraps" will get "knit up" so they disappear and the gap will close.

To knit up the wraps: Knit to a wrapped stitch. Insert the right needle under the wrap on the *knit side* and knit it together with the stitch it is wrapped around.

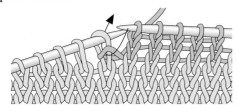

On the purl side of the work: Purl to the designated stitch. Slip the next stitch from the left needle to the right needle as if to purl. Move the yarn between the needles to the back. Slip the stitch back to the left needle. Move the yarn to the front. Don't pull the yarn too tightly. Turn the work and knit back across the stitches that were previously purled. Continue in this manner until all short rows are worked. It will look like there is yarn wrapped around a stitch in a manner that resembles a purl bar. There will also be a small gap between the stitches on the needle where the turn was made. On subsequent rows the "wraps" will get "purled up" so they disappear and the gap will close.

To purl up the wraps: Purl to a wrapped stitch. Insert the needle under the wrap on the *knit side* and purl it together with the stitch it is wrapped around. This is a little awkward. The stitches can be pulled over one at a time.

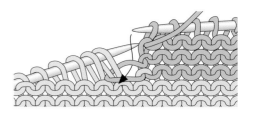

Bind Offs

Traditional bind off (BO): Knit 2 stitches. *Insert left needle into the first stitch on the right needle. Pull this stitch over the second stitch and off the right needle. One stitch remains on the right needle. Knit the next stitch. Repeat from * until all stitches are bound off.

Partial-row bind off or lace bind off: This method is used to bind off a partial row and is not always indicated in a pattern. Once you know how and when to use it, you can use it instead of a normal bind off. It is used in the Textured Squares Scarf and the Textured Squares Mohair Shawl. *Knit two stitches together. Place the resulting stitch back on the left needle. Repeat from * until required number of stitches are bound off. Do not place the last stitch from the bind off on the left needle before continuing with the directions. Proceed with directions for row.

FRINGE BASICS

CUT A PIECE of heavy cardboard to the dimensions indicated in the pattern and cut a small slit at one edge. Using the number of strands of yarn specified in the pattern, insert the end of yarn into the slit and wrap the yarns loosely around the cardboard. When the cardboard gets full, cut the yarn at the end of the cardboard with the slit. Cut across the yarns at the end of the cardboard where you started and ended the yarns. Gently remove the yarn from the cardboard.

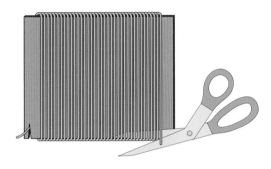

NOTE: *Do not wind too much yarn onto the cardboard; otherwise the fringe wrapped over a large amount of previously wrapped yarn will end up being longer than the fringe wrapped at the beginning. Your fringe will not be all the same length and will have to be trimmed.*

Taking the appropriate number of strands, fold them in half and make a loop. Insert a large crochet hook from underneath into the appropriate hole or stitch in the knitting and pull the loop to the right side. Do not pull the loop all the way through. Make the loop big enough so you can pull the ends of yarn through the loop and pull down snugly. Repeat for as many fringes as required, winding more fringe if necessary.

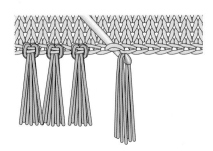

TASSEL BASICS

SEE "FRINGE BASICS" for winding and cutting yarn. Wind and cut a quantity of yarn appropriate for the tassel size you want. Holding all of the strands together, fold them in half and tie a 12" strand of yarn in the middle. Use a crochet hook to pull one of the ends of yarn through the designated area in the garment. Tie the two ends together and tuck them into the middle of the tassel. Tightly wrap a 20" strand of yarn about 1" from the top. Use a crochet hook to pull the ends under the wrap.

GAUGE

DIRECTIONS ALWAYS SAY, "To save time, take the time to knit a gauge." So you are thinking, "Hmm, how does that save me time when what I really want to do is start knitting this wonderful pattern?" The idea is that if you knit the gauge swatch and make sure the gauge is correct, you won't have the disappointment of having to rip out a garment that doesn't fit and start over. Yikes, what an awful thought.

Let's say the pattern gauge says 20 stitches equals 4". While 4" is the standard size swatch used in patterns, you should really knit a sample swatch at least 6" to 8" to get a true average of your knitting. Most knitters get pretty relaxed after knitting on a project for awhile, which could change the gauge. The original swatch should be in that relaxed state of knitting as well. The bigger the swatch and the longer it takes you to knit it, the truer the gauge will be. This also gives you a chance to get the feel of the yarn and the pattern stitch if there is one.

So you take the time and knit the gauge, but it is only a little tiny bit off. It won't make that much difference, or will it? The answer is a resounding "yes." Let's do the math so you can see just how much difference it makes. Let's say you are supposed to get five stitches to the inch and you get four and a half stitches instead. It's just a tiny bit off, right? The piece of knitting you are going to work requires one hundred stitches. You divide one hundred by the five stitches to the inch you were supposed to get: the piece should measure 20" across when completed. When you divide the hundred stitches by the four and a half stitches per inch that you got in your sample, the piece will now measure 22¼". That means your knitting would be 2¼" too big. If you were knitting a sweater that was supposed to measure a total of 40" at five stitches to the inch, it would measure 44½" at four and a half stitches to the inch. That is quite a bit larger than was intended.

Don't get a false sense of security when knitting an item that doesn't have to "fit" quite so accurately. Sometimes people think that stitch gauge doesn't matter with a scarf or a shawl or maybe an afghan. So what if it comes out a little bigger? Right, so what? The item could also come out too small if your gauge is too tight. And if it is too loose, you could run out of yarn or end up with something that has to wrap around your body twice so it doesn't drag on the floor.

Row gauge is very difficult to match from knitter to knitter, but it is a little more lenient as far as affecting the overall size of the garment. Most of the knitting we do is measured in inches, not rows, so we can usually be a little off on the row gauge and still come out okay. The real problem is that neck shaping and sleeve increases (in garments with sleeves) are all calculated using the given row gauge, so if yours doesn't match, the neck could end up too large or the sleeves too long.

The final issue about gauge is that if yours doesn't match the pattern, your yarn usage could differ from the quantity listed in the pattern. That means you could run out or have too much. Usually the problem is that you run out and then have to find one last skein in the same dye lot—generally impossible if you've had the yarn for a while. If your gauge is correct and you've purchased enough yarn, you shouldn't run out.

To make sure you have the right amount of yarn, always buy based on yardage, not ounces. Most yarns today, if not all, have the yardage listed on the label. If the yarn you want does not, refer to a book that provides yardage. Your yarn retailer should be able to help you.

Let's see why yardage is more accurate than ounces. A 50-gram or 1.75-ounce skein of yarn has about 110 yards if it is cotton and about 130 to 140 yards if it is wool. Cotton is heavier, so in weighing yarn you are going to get fewer yards per ounce if it is cotton than if it is wool. If you know the yardage on a skein of yarn, you can then use it to calculate how much to buy instead of using the weight.

Here is the math:

The pattern requires 10 skeins of cotton yarn at 110 yards per skein. 10 x 110 = 1,100 yards.

The yarn you are purchasing has 140 yards per skein.

1,100 ÷ 140 = 7.85 skeins. You can't buy .85 of a skein, so you need 8 skeins to get the correct yardage plus a little extra.

Some people like to buy extra "just in case." It doesn't hurt, and you'll end up with extra to add to the stash. Or if you decide to make the garment a little longer or bigger, you'll have enough yarn.

ABBREVIATIONS

beg	Begin/beginning	p2sso	Pass 2 slip stitches over
BO	Bind off	pw	Purlwise
CC Dec	Central chain decrease	RS	Right side
ch	Chain	RSR	Right side row
circ	Circular	sc	Single crochet
CO	Cast on	sl	Slip
cont	Continue	SSK	Slip, slip, knit
dec	Decrease	SSSK	Slip, slip, slip, knit
dpn	Double-pointed needle	SSP	Slip, slip, purl
EOR	Every other row	st(s)	Stitch(es)
inc	Increase	st st	Stockinette stitch
K	Knit	W and T	Wrap and turn
K2tog	Knit 2 together	wyib	With yarn in back
kw	Knitwise	wyif	With yarn in front
M1	Make 1 increase	WS	Wrong side
P	Purl	WSR	Wrong side row
psso	Pass slip stitch over	YO	Yarn over

NOTE: *Sometimes you will see these abbreviations in parentheses. Do everything inside the parentheses the number of times indicated outside the parentheses. For example, (K1, P1) 3 times means to knit 1, purl 1, knit 1, purl 1, knit 1, purl 1.*

BASIC SHAPED SHAWL

THE BASIC SHAPE of a shawl has always been a triangle, a square, or a rectangle with some occasional variations. The stole has tended to be a rectangle of various widths and lengths. The scarf has ranged in size from long rectangles over 8' long and 10" wide to average rectangles measuring approximately 8" by 50" to 60" long. All of them appear to have straight edges and no neck shaping or shaping in the body.

To me, it doesn't make much sense to force a flat piece of rectangular fabric around the body. It makes more sense to shape the piece around the body, or to make places for the neck and head. The following illustration shows some of the shapes that I use to make shawls and scarves fit better.

Shawl or scarf with   A circular shawl shaped
back neck shaping   with short rows

Knitters don't have to have shawls and scarves that grab and bunch up at the neck or hang unevenly at the edges, because we can put shaping in as we knit. The possibilities are endless when you think of all the different techniques available for creating a better fitting knitted garment:

- Increases and decreases

- Short row shaping

- Knitted patterns that drape: cables, ribbing, garter stitch

- Yarn overs creating lace or texture

- Individual motifs that can be worked separately for color, texture, shaping, and placement

A good example of a better-shaped shawl, the Sideways Shawl is the basic triangular shawl knit in an unusual way. It is knit in garter stitch on big needles with two different weights and textures of yarns. Yarn overs are included along one edge to create holes for the fringe. It has shaping at the back neck to make it stay on the shoulders and fit around the front of the body.

The usual way to knit this shawl would be to start at the point and increase toward the neck. Instead, this shawl is made starting at the side and increasing to the neck, where the neck is shaped. The other side is the mirror image of the first side and is done by working decreases. This is a very simple shawl with a beautiful drape and fit.

SIDEWAYS SHAWL

MATERIALS

2 skeins of Mountain Colors Mohair (78% mohair, 13% wool, 9% nylon, 225yds/4oz); color Columbine

5 skeins of Mountain Colors Moguls (98% wool, 2% nylon, 65yds/4oz); color Columbine

Size 11 US (8mm) circular needle (29"), or size required to obtain gauge

8" by 10" piece of cardboard for fringe

Gauge: 12 sts and 16 rows = 4" in garter stitch, alternating yarns every 2 rows

DIRECTIONS

Note: *Work two rows using each yarn. Carry yarn not in use loosely up the edge; do not cut.*

CO 2 sts using Moguls, K across. Change to Mohair, (RS) K1, YO, K1. K 1 row. Change to Moguls, K2, YO, K1. K 1 row. Change to Mohair, K3, YO, K1. K 1 row. Change to Moguls, K4, YO, K1. K 1 row. Cont inc in this manner, alternating the 2 yarns every 2 rows and working a YO 1 st from end of each RS row. Knit all WS rows. When straight edge measures 30" from CO (or, if you desire a wider shawl, when it measures the desired size), beg neck shaping as follows: BO 3 sts at beg of next 4 RS rows. Cont to place YO 1 st from end of row. Work without further neck shaping for 3". Beg reverse shaping by working to 5 sts from end of row, K2tog twice, YO, K1 at end of every RS row. Work another 3" at back neck, then CO 3 sts at beg of next 4 RS rows. Cont reverse shaping until 2 sts remain. Ending with Moguls, BO.

(diagram) 30"

Direction of knitting

FINISHING

Weave in all ends. Add fringe. Holding Moguls and Mohair together, wrap both yarns around the 8" width of cardboard. Cut 1 end. Using 1 strand of each yarn held together, insert fringe into each YO along the bottom edge. See "Fringe Basics" page 11.

DIAGONAL KNITTING

THE CONCEPT OF diagonal knitting is rather intriguing. By simply working an increase at one end of a row and a decrease at the other end of the row, you give the knitted piece a completely different shape. Instead of forming horizontal and vertical lines, the knitting slants on the diagonal. This gives a whole new look to the knitting and basic stitch patterns. For example, a textured square no longer looks like a square. Because it sits on the diagonal, it looks more like a diamond. You can work any simple pattern on the diagonal as long as you can keep it in the correct sequence, working the increases and decreases at the beginning and end of the row.

The diagonal knit scarf represented in this technique uses a simple knit two, purl two pattern. This stitch pattern doesn't require a border to keep it flat, so it's perfect for the scarf. If you want to add a border, place the diagonal-knitting increases and decreases before and after the border stitches.

I could have worked the pattern for the length of the scarf, producing a diagonally knit straight piece. But, to add interest and make the scarf fit better, I reversed the shaping at the back of the neck. Remember when I talked about shaping scarves to fit the neck so they rest on the shoulders and don't fall off? Simply stated, the basic pattern would read as follows without the pattern stitch. It's the pattern stitch you choose that adds even more interest to the scarf.

CO any number of stitches. Increase 1 stitch at the beginning of the row, and decrease at the end of the row. Work 1 row without increases or decreases. Repeat these 2 rows until piece is desired length. Reverse shaping by decreasing 1 stitch at the beginning of the row and increasing at the end of the row. Work 1 row without increases or decreases. Repeat these 2 rows until desired length. Bind off.

While the shaping on the Diagonal Scarf looks the same as that used on the Chenille Diagonal Lace Scarf, it is the result of a different technique. On the Diagonal Scarf, the diagonal shape is formed by the position of the increases and decreases in each row. For the first half of the scarf, the increases are worked at the beginning of the row and the decreases are worked at the end of the row. For the second half of the scarf, the increases and decreases are done on opposite sides: decreases at the beginning and increases at the end.

The diagonal shaping of the Chenille Diagonal Lace Scarf is a result of the direction of the decreases in the knitting pattern. The first half of the scarf is shaped using K2tog across the row, which causes the piece to slant to the right. The second half is worked using SSK across the row, which causes the piece to slant to the left. A yarn over is placed next to the decrease to keep the stitch number the same. So we can get the same effect as the Diagonal Scarf by simply letting the pattern stitch in the Chenille Diagonal Lace Scarf do the work of creating the diagonal knitting. Pretty nifty.

DIAGONAL SCARF

MATERIALS

3 skeins of Kid Slique by Prism (50% rayon,
   50% kid mohair, 88yds/2oz); color Arroyo
Size 8 US (5mm) knitting needles, or size
   required to obtain gauge

Gauge: 16 sts and 24 rows = 4" in pattern

PATTERN STITCH

(Multiple of 4 sts plus 2)
Rows 1 and 4: (K2, P2) across, end K2.
Rows 2 and 3: (P2, K2) across, end P2.

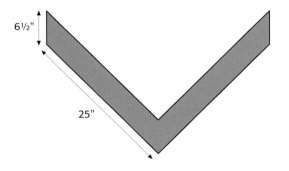

DIRECTIONS

CO 38 sts. Work pattern stitch for 1 row. Next row (RS) and every RS row, inc (M1) at beg of row and dec (K2tog) at end of row. Keeping continuity of pattern stitch, work WS rows without inc or dec.

When work measures 25" along one long edge and ends with a row 1 or row 3, cont as above except dec (SSK) at beg and inc (M1) at end of even-numbered rows. When 2 sides are the same length, BO loosely.

FINISHING

Weave in all ends. Steam gently.

CHENILLE DIAGONAL LACE SCARF

MATERIALS

3 skeins of Crystal Palace Cotton Chenille
(100% cotton, 98yds/50g); color 4021
Size 7 US (4.5mm) knitting needles, or size
required to obtain gauge

Gauge: 16 sts and 24 rows = 4" in garter
stitch

DIRECTIONS

CO 40 sts, K5 rows.
Row 1: K4, (YO, K2tog) to last 4 sts, K4.
Row 2: K4, P to last 4 sts, K4.
Repeat rows 1 and 2 until work measures 26".
Row 3: K4, (SSK, YO) to last 4 sts, K4.
Row 4: K4, P to last 4 sts, K4.
Repeat rows 3 and 4 until work measures 25" from
pattern change at back neck.
K 5 rows. BO loosely.

FINISHING

Weave in all ends. Steam gently.

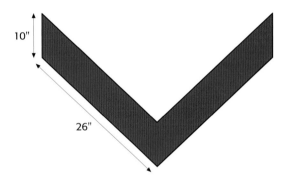

TEXTURED PATTERNS

ANY COMBINATION OF knit and purl stitches will yield a wonderful textured pattern. These patterns are often more interesting to knit than stockinette stitch, and they usually don't change the gauge a lot. There are many patterns to choose from. Most people think of a simple ribbing pattern first, but the possibilities are endless. The embossed look of scattered purl stitches on a knit background is simply delightful to work and generally easy to memorize, as the knitter can see what is happening while knitting the pattern.

Often textured patterns do not have a specific right or wrong side, so they are the perfect choice for garments where either side might show. The Textured Squares Scarf and the Textured Squares Mohair Shawl are good examples of the way these wonderful patterns work. They are both made with a series of squares using stockinette, reverse stockinette, and garter stitch. They are also knit on the diagonal with shaping at the back neck to make them stay on the shoulders better. The patterns are extremely interesting to knit and will give you a better understanding of a simple knit and purl pattern that changes frequently.

While knitting textured patterns, take care that the working yarn does not loop over the needle when you move it to the correct side to be worked. If it loops over the needle, it can look like another stitch. The stitch patterns usually flow easily once you learn them. Count the stitches in the different sections on a regular basis to make sure that you haven't inadvertently added stitches to the pattern. By the way, working different pattern stitches uses up more yarn than working a straight stockinette stitch, because moving the yarn from the knit position or purl position leaves yarn sitting between stitches.

Sometimes charts are used to show these patterns. The charts may rely on the knitter's understanding of what forms a stitch. In stockinette stitch, if a purl stitch is to show on the right side of the knitting, it must be worked as a knit stitch on the wrong side. In other words: a knit is the front of a purl, and a purl is the back of a knit. Think about it; it's not as complicated as it sounds.

Textured Squares Scarf

MATERIALS

4 skeins of Sportlife by GGH from Muench
    Yarns (100% wool, 93yds/50g); color 38
Size 8 US (5mm) knitting needles, or size
    required to obtain gauge

Gauge: 16 sts and 24 rows = 4" in stockinette
    stitch

DIRECTIONS

Section 1
CO 6 sts, K 10 rows.

Section 2
Row 1: (RS) CO 6 sts, K12.
Row 2: CO 6 sts, K6, P6, K6; 18 sts.
Row 3: K18.
Row 4: K6, P6, K6.
(Repeat rows 3 and 4) 3 times.

Section 3
Row 1: CO 6 sts, K12, P6, K6.
Row 2: CO 6 sts, K6, (P6, K6) twice; 30 sts.
Row 3: K12, P6, K12.
Row 4: K6, (P6, K6) twice.
(Repeat rows 3 and 4) 3 times.

Section 4
Row 1: CO 6 sts, K12, (P6, K6) twice.
Row 2: CO 6 sts, K6, (P6, K6) 3 times; 42 sts.
Row 3: K12, P6, K6, P6, K12.
Row 4: (K6, P6) 3 times, K6.
(Repeat rows 3 and 4) 3 times.

Section 5
Use the partial-row bind off on page 10. The last
stitch left on the right needle from binding off
counts as the first stitch of the number of stitches
you are directed to work next.

Row 1: CO 6 sts, K12, P6, K6, P6, K18.
Row 2: BO 6, (K6, P6) 3 times, K6; 42 sts.
Row 3: K12, P6, K6, P6, K12.
Row 4: (K6, P6) 3 times, K6.
(Repeat rows 3 and 4) 3 times.
(Repeat section 5) 10 times.

At center back, reverse shaping as follows:

Section 6
Row 1: BO 6 sts, K12, P6, K18.
Row 2: CO 6 sts. (K6, P6) 3 times, K6; 42 sts.
Row 3: K12, P6, K6, P6, K12.
Row 4: (K6, P6) 3 times, K6.
(Repeat rows 3 and 4) 3 times.
(Repeat section 6) 10 times.

Section 7
Row 1: BO 6 sts, K12, P6, K18.
Row 2: BO 6 sts, (K6, P6) twice, K6; 30 sts.
Row 3: K12, P6, K12.
Row 4: (K6, P6) twice, K6.
(Repeat rows 3 and 4) 3 times.

Section 8

Row 1: BO 6 sts, K24.

Row 2: BO 6 sts, K6, P6, K6; 18 sts.

Row 3: K18.

Row 4: K6, P6, K6.

(Repeat rows 3 and 4) 3 times.

Section 9

Row 1: BO 6 sts, K12.

Row 2: BO 6 sts, K6; 6 sts.

Row 3: K6.

Row 4: K6.

(Repeat rows 3 and 4) 3 times. BO all sts.

FINISHING

Weave in all ends. Steam gently.

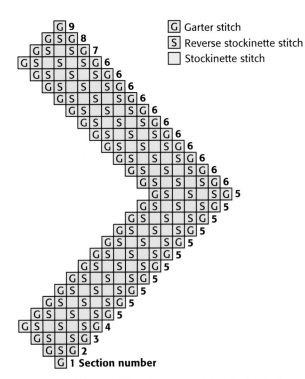

	G	Garter stitch
	S	Reverse stockinette stitch
		Stockinette stitch

Pattern stitches within each square with right side facing

TEXTURED SQUARES
MOHAIR SHAWL

This shawl is an adaptation of the Textured Squares Scarf. The pattern is the same
except for the number of stitches and repeats of the pattern.

MATERIALS

3 skeins of Mountain Colors Mohair (78% mohair, 13% wool, 9% nylon, 225yds/4oz); color Sierra

Size 10½ US (6.5mm) knitting needle or size required to obtain gauge

Gauge: 14 sts and 16 rows = 4" in stockinette stitch

DIRECTIONS

Section 1
CO 5 sts, K 8 rows.

Section 2
Row 1: (RS) CO 5 sts, K10.
Row 2: CO 5 sts, K5, P5, K5; 15 sts.
Row 3: K15.
Row 4: K5, P5, K5.
(Repeat rows 3 and 4) twice.

Section 3
Row 1: CO 5 sts, K10, P5, K5.
Row 2: CO 5 sts, K5, (P5, K5) twice; 25 sts.
Row 3: K10, P5, K10.
Row 4: (K5, P5) twice, K5.
(Repeat rows 3 and 4) twice.

Section 4
Row 1: CO 5 sts, K10, (P5, K5) twice.
Row 2: CO 5 sts, K5 (P5, K5) 3 times; 35 sts.
Row 3: K10, (P5, K5) twice, K5.
Row 4: (K5, P5) 3 times, K5.
(Repeat rows 3 and 4) twice.

Section 5
Row 1: CO 5 sts, K10, (P5, K5) 3 times.
Row 2: CO 5 sts, K5, (P5, K5) 4 times; 45 sts.
Row 3: K10, (P5, K5) 3 times, K5.
Row 4: K5, (P5, K5) 4 times.
(Repeat rows 3 and 4) twice.

Section 6
Row 1: CO 5 sts, K10, (P5, K5) 4 times.
Row 2: CO 5 sts, K5, (P5, K5) 5 times; 55 sts.
Row 3: K10, (P5, K5) 4 times, K5.
Row 4: K5, (P5, K5) 5 times.
(Repeat rows 3 and 4) twice.

Section 7
Row 1: CO 5 sts, K10 (P5, K5) 5 times.
Row 2: CO 5 sts, K5, (P5, K5) 6 times; 65 sts.
Row 3: K10, (P5, K5) 5 times, K5.
Row 4: K5, (P5, K5) 6 times.
(Repeat rows 3 and 4) twice.

Section 8
Row 1: CO 5 sts, K10 (P5, K5) 6 times.
Row 2: CO 5 sts, K5, (P5, K5) 7 times; 75 sts.
Row 3: K10, (P5, K5) 6 times, K5.
Row 4: K5, (P5, K5) 7 times.
(Repeat rows 3 and 4) twice.

Section 9
Row 1: CO 5 sts, K10 (P5, K5) 7 times.
Row 2: CO 5 sts, K5, (P5, K5) 8 times; 85 sts.
Row 3: K10, (P5, K5) 7 times, K5.
Row 4: K5, (P5, K5) 8 times.
(Repeat rows 3 and 4) twice.

Section 10
Row 1: CO 5 sts, K10 (P5, K5) 8 times.
Row 2: CO 5 sts, K5, (P5, K5) 9 times; 95 sts.
Row 3: K10, (P5, K5) 8 times, K5.
Row 4: K5, (P5, K5) 9 times.
(Repeat rows 3 and 4) twice.

Section 11

Use the partial-row bind off on page 10. The last stitch left on the right needle from binding off counts as the first stitch of the number of stitches you are directed to work next.

Row 1: CO 5 sts, K10 (P5, K5) 8 times, K10.
Row 2: BO 5 sts, K5, (P5, K5) 9 times; 95 sts.
Row 3: K10, (P5, K5) 8 times, K5.
Row 4: K5, (P5, K5) 9 times.
(Repeat rows 3 and 4) twice.
(Repeat section 11) 8 times.

At center back, reverse shaping as follows:

Section 12

Row 1: BO 5 sts, K10, (P5, K5) 8 times.
Row 2: CO 5 sts, K5, (P5, K5) 9 times; 95 sts.
Row 3: K10, (P5, K5) 8 times, K5.
Row 4: (K5, P5) 9 times, K5.
(Repeat rows 3 and 4) twice.
(Repeat section 12) 8 times.

Section 13

Row 1: BO 5 sts, K10, (P5, K5) 7 times, K10.
Row 2: BO 5 sts, (K5, P5) 8 times, K5; 85 sts.
Row 3: K10, (P5, K5) 7 times, K5.
Row 4: K5, (P5, K5) 8 times.
(Repeat rows 3 and 4) twice.

Section 14

Row 1: BO 5 sts, K10, (P5, K5) 6 times, K10.
Row 2: BO 5 sts, (K5, P5) 7 times, K5; 75 sts.
Row 3: K10, (P5, K5) 6 times, K5.
Row 4: K5, (P5, K5) 7 times.
(Repeat rows 3 and 4) twice.

Section 15

Row 1: BO 5 sts, K10, (P5, K5) 5 times, K10.
Row 2: BO 5 sts, (K5, P5) 6 times, K5; 65 sts.
Row 3: K10, (P5, K5) 5 times, K5.
Row 4: K5, (P5, K5) 6 times.
(Repeat rows 3 and 4) twice.

Section 16

Row 1: BO 5 sts, K10, (P5, K5) 4 times, K10.
Row 2: BO 5 sts, (K5, P5) 5 times, K5; 55 sts.
Row 3: K10, (P5, K5) 4 times, K5.
Row 4: K5, (P5, K5) 5 times.
(Repeat rows 3 and 4) twice.

Section 17

Row 1: BO 5 sts, K10, (P5, K5) 3 times, K10.
Row 2: BO 5 sts, (K5, P5) 4 times, K5; 45 sts.
Row 3: K10, (P5, K5) 3 times, K5.
Row 4: K5, (P5, K5) 4 times.
(Repeat rows 3 and 4) twice.

Section 18

Row 1: BO 5 sts, K10, (P5, K5) twice, K10.
Row 2: BO 5 sts, (K5, P5) 3 times, K5; 35 sts.
Row 3: K10, (P5, K5) twice, K5.
Row 4: K5, (P5, K5) 3 times.
(Repeat rows 3 and 4) twice.

Section 19

Row 1: BO 5 sts, K10, P5, K15.
Row 2: BO 5 sts, (K5, P5) twice, K5; 25 sts.
Row 3: K10, P5, K10.
Row 4: K5, (P5, K5) twice.
(Repeat rows 3 and 4) twice.

Section 20

Row 1: BO 5 sts, K20.
Row 2: BO 5 sts, K5, P5 K5; 15 sts.
Row 3: K15.
Row 4: K5, P5, K5.
(Repeat rows 3 and 4) twice.

Section 21

Row 1: BO 5 sts, K10.
Row 2: BO 5 sts, K5; 5 sts.
Row 3: K5.
Row 4: K5.
(Repeat rows 3 and 4) twice.
BO all sts.

FINISHING

Weave in all ends. Steam gently if necessary.

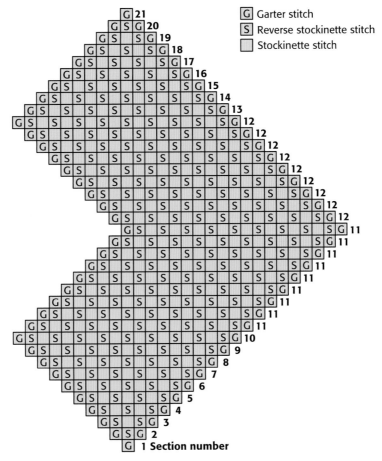

G	Garter stitch
S	Reverse stockinette stitch
	Stockinette stitch

Pattern stitches within each square with right side facing

SLIP STITCHES

Slip stitching is one of the simplest forms of color knitting. It varies from other color techniques for these reasons:

- Only one color is used across a row.

- Yarn does not need to be cut, but simply carried up the side of the work, so you weave in fewer ends.

- Yarns of different weight, texture, or fiber content can be mixed for different effects.

- The knitting terminology related to slip stitches is very simple.

Garments made with slip stitches are by far some of the easiest to work. The slip stitches result in a wonderful piece of fabric that is very comfortable to wear. You may have to work with more stitches across a row than you would in stockinette stitch, but the patterns are fun to knit, so you won't mind or even notice. The reason for needing more stitches is that sometimes the slipped stitches sit on top of the background color and don't add, or add very little, width to the piece of knitting. The gauge swatch to test the patterns will give you this information. Just be sure to count all the stitches when measuring the gauge, not just the ones that are making the piece get larger. Do not measure the gauge on the back of the swatch.

You'll find a variety of slip stitch patterns in the many stitch pattern books available today.

Although they often show up better in two colors, some amazing things can happen if slip stitch patterns are worked in one color or in a variegated yarn. You may also see another variation of slip stitches called mosaic patterns. The concept is similar, with one color worked across a row at a time, but the mosaic patterns seem to resemble a garter stitch texture when you look at them. The wrong side row in mosaic patterns will also be the same as the right side row, which is not always the case in slip stitch patterns.

The Slip Stitch Stole pattern was much simpler to design than the Slip Stitch Sampler Scarf pattern. For the stole I chose a pattern that, when knit with the two very different weights and textures of yarn, made a very pleasing and drapey fabric. The "puffiness" of the chenille is caused by the single slip stitch for four rows in the ribbon and the fact that the two yarns are of two different weights. It is a most pleasing way to use two very different yarns. See page 8 for more on slip stitches.

To design the Slip Stitch Sampler Scarf, I went through many stitch pattern books and looked for slip stitch patterns that looked interesting and fun to knit. I then narrowed down the choices to patterns that looked horizontal and vertical. I wanted to be able to alternate the patterns in the scarf to add more interest to the design.

I then chose patterns where only one stitch is slipped at a time to keep the gauge the same or similar. This also eliminates the long floats on the back of the work that would look unsightly if the scarf were turned over. The patterns also had to have multiples of stitches that would work out to the same number for each section. I could have increased or decreased to make them work if necessary, but I was hoping I wouldn't have to do that. Once the patterns were all chosen, I sat down and knit a sample of all of them to be sure the gauge would stay the same so the scarf would have straight edges. The border pattern is from a sweater I had designed previously.

After knitting the swatches, I arranged them in what I thought would be the most pleasing order. Having actual swatches to move around made it easier to see what the scarf would look like than if I had worked with the pictures in the stitch pattern books. I also had to make sure the patterns would look the same—or similar enough—on the side of the scarf where I cast on as on the side where I cast off. When the scarf draped around someone's neck, one side would hang upside down compared to the other side. Once I was pleased with all of that, I was ready to knit. I wasn't sure how big each section was going to be, but I purposely chose the thicker, more densely knit section for the back of the neck, where I felt most of the warmth would be needed. The rest just fell into place.

SLIP STITCH STOLE

MATERIALS

5 skeins of Great Adirondack Chamois
(80% rayon, 20% cotton, 100yds/50g);
color Lotus

5 skeins of Great Adirondack Metallica (85%
rayon, 15% metallic polyester, 100yds/50g);
color Lotus

Size 8 US (5mm) knitting needles, or size
required to obtain gauge

Crochet hook, size G

Gauge: 16 sts and 32 rows = 4" in slip-stitch
pattern

DIRECTIONS

NOTE: *Carry yarns not in use loosely up the side. Do not cut.*

CO 52 sts using Metallica, P 1 row.
Rows 1 and 3: Change to Chamois, K3, sl 1, (K4, sl 1) 9 times, K3.
Rows 2 and 4: P3, sl 1, (P4, sl 1) 9 times, P3.
Rows 5 and 7: Change to Metallica, K across.
Rows 6 and 8: P across.
Repeat rows 1 through 8 until work measures 71" or desired length, ending with row 6. BO loosely.

Edging

Using crochet hook and Chamois and starting at a corner on RS, work along the long edge of the shawl as follows: work 4 double crochets in center of Chamois section, 1 single crochet in center of Metallica section. Work 4 double crochets in corners. Continue pattern around entire edge of shawl. Join with a slip stitch.

Using Metallica, work one single crochet in each stitch around entire edge. Join with a slip stitch. Do not turn. Work one row of backward single crochet in each st around. Join with a slip stitch. Finish off.

FINISHING

Weave in all ends. Steam gently. Corners should be rounded but lie flat.

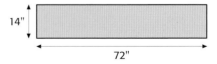

SLIP STITCH SAMPLER SCARF

MATERIALS

Color A: 4 skeins of Karabella Yarns Aurora 8 (100% merino wool, 98yds/50g); color 3, purple

Color B: 4 skeins of Karabella Yarns Aurora 8; color 11, green

Size 7 US (4.5mm) knitting needles, or size required to obtain gauge

2 ring markers

Gauge: 18 sts and 24 rows = 4" in stockinette stitch

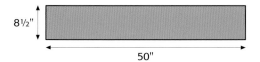

8½"

50"

DIRECTIONS

NOTE: *Twist yarns at side edge when changing colors by moving the color you are dropping to the back and pulling the new color up loosely from the front. Do not cut yarns.*

CO 45 sts using color A. Work 2 rows as follows in rib.

Row 1: (K1, P1) across, end K1.

Row 2: (P1, K1) across, end P1.

Pattern 1 for top and bottom borders

Row 1: K1 (K1 in stitch below [see page 9], P1) across, end K1.

Row 2: Using A, K to end.

Row 3: Using B, K1, (P1, K1 in stitch below) across, end K1.

Row 4: Using B, K to end.

Repeat rows 1 through 4 once, then rows 1 and 2 once.

For the remainder of the knitting, keep 5 sts at each end in pattern 1 to form border of scarf. Place a marker after the first 5 sts and before the last 5 sts. The center 35 sts will be worked in the different patterns as follows. Only the directions for the center sts will be given. Use the following directions for the edge stitches only:

Pattern 1 for first 5 stitches on right side (with RS facing you).

Row 1: Using B, K1, (P1, K1 in stitch below) twice.

Row 2: Using B, K5.

Row 3: Using A, K1 (K1 in stitch below, P1) twice.

Row 4: Using A, K5.

Repeat rows 1 through 4.

Pattern 1 for last 5 stitches on left side (with RS facing you).

Row 1: Using B, (K1 in stitch below, P1) twice, K1.

Row 2: Using B, K5.

Row 3: Using A, (P1, K1 in stitch below) twice, K1.

Row 4: Using A, K5.

Repeat rows 1 through 4.

Pattern 2

Row 1: Using B, K1, (sl 1 wyib, K1, sl 1 wyib, K3) repeat across, end last repeat with K1.

Row 2: Using B, K1, (sl 1 wyif, K1, sl 1 wyif, P3) to last 4 sts, end (sl 1, K1) twice.

Row 3: Using A, K1, (K3, sl 1 wyib, K1, sl 1 wyib) repeat to last 4 sts, end K4.

Row 4: Using A, K1, (P3, sl 1 wyif, K1, sl 1 wyif) to last 4 sts, end P3, K1.

Repeat rows 1 through 4 of Pattern 2 for 4 1/2". Repeat rows 1 and 2 once.

K across using A.

Pattern 3

Row 1 (WS): Using A, P across.

Row 2: Using B, K3, (sl 1 wyib, K3) to end.

Row 3: Using B, K3, (sl 1 wyif, K3) to end.

Row 4: Using A, K1 (sl 1 wyib, K3) to last 2 sts, end sl 1, K1.

Row 5: Using A, K1 (sl 1 wyif, K3) to last 2 sts, end sl 1, K1.

Row 6: Using B, repeat row 2.

Row 7: Using B, repeat row 3.

Row 8: Using A, repeat row 4.

Repeat rows 1 through 8 of pattern 3 for 5". Repeat row 1 once using A.

Pattern 4

Row 1: Using B, K1 (sl 1 wyib, K1) to end.

Row 2: Using B, K1 (sl 1 wyif, K1) to end.

Rows 3 and 4: Using A, K across.

Row 5: Using B, K2 (sl 1 wyib, K1) to last st, K1.

Row 6: Using B, K2, (sl 1 wyif, K1) to last st, K1.

Row 7: Using A, K across.

Row 8: Using A, K across.

Repeat rows 1 through 8 of Pattern 4 for 4½". Repeat rows 1 through 6 once.

Pattern 5

Row 1: Using A, K3, (sl 1 wyib, K3) to end.

Row 2: Using A, K3, (sl 1 wyif, K3) to end.

Row 3: Using B, K1, (sl 1 wyib, K3) to last 2 sts, end sl 1, K1.

Row 4: Using B, K1, (sl 1 wyif, K3) to last 2 sts, end sl 1, K1.

Repeat rows 1 through 4 of Pattern 5 for 5".

Pattern 6 (center back)

Row 1: Using A, K1, (sl 1 wyib, K1) to end.

Row 2: Using A, K1 (sl 1 wyif, K1) to end.

Rows 3 and 4: Using B, K to end.

Row 5: Using A, K1, (sl 1 wyib, K1) to end.

Row 6: Using A, P1 (sl 1 wyif, P1) to end.

Repeat rows 3 through 6 of Pattern 6 for 8", repeat rows 1 and 2 once.

Repeat the patterns as follows to form the opposite side of the scarf.

Pattern 5: Work rows 3 and 4 once, repeat rows 1 through 4 until section measures 5".

Pattern 4: Work rows 7 and 8 once, repeat rows 1 through 8 until section measures 5".

Pattern 3: Work rows 2 through 8 once, repeat rows 1 through 8 until section measures 5". K across using A.

Pattern 2: Repeat rows 1 through 4 for 4½", then rows 1 and 2 once.

Pattern 1: Repeat rows 1 through 4 twice. Using A, work next 2 rows in rib as follows:
Row 1: (K1, P1) across, end K1.
Row 2: (P1, K1) across, end P1.
BO loosely.

FINISHING

Weave in all ends and block gently. Pattern 1 on the sides will flare slightly until blocked.

CABLES

CABLES OFTEN BRING fear to the souls of knitters new and old. Once they learn how to knit them, people usually say something like "That was so simple, I don't know why I didn't try them sooner." Simply stated: you knit cables by changing the order in which the stitches are knit. Using a third needle known as a "cable needle" to hold the stitches, you move certain stitches to the back or to the front of the work and knit them in a different order. To my mind, once you've learned to turn or twist one cable, you know how to work all cables.

There are lots of cable variations. Some twist to the back, some twist to the front, and some use more than one cable needle, but honestly the process is the same. It's amazing how simply changing the order in which stitches are knit can create such beautiful textured patterns.

Cable needles range from fancy needles with a notch in the middle to ones that are bent like a horseshoe. Even a simple, double-pointed sock needle will work, especially a short one that measures about 4" to 5". The stitches are on the cable needle for only a moment, so it doesn't have to be fancy, although some styles of cable needles tend to be easier for some people to use. The most important thing about a cable needle is that it has a point at each end. I've even resorted to using a toothpick if I was traveling and didn't have anything else that would work. It is also wise to use a cable needle a bit smaller than the knitting needle used for the garment so the stitches don't get

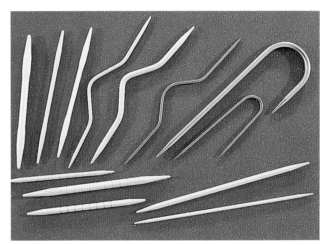

Cable needles

enlarged as they are held on the cable needle and moved to their new position.

Very heavily patterned sweaters with lots of cables are some of the most interesting garments you'll find to make. Cables not only look beautiful, but they impress even the most experienced knitters.

Cables tend to be in columns. Often one cable will have a different number of rows than another cable, so you really need to keep track of the rows while knitting these patterns. It is possible that you could be working row 6 of one pattern, row 22 of another pattern, and row 12 of a third pattern, all within one row. Placing ring markers on the needle to separate the patterns will help you know when a different pattern is about to start. Keeping track with pencil and paper might be the best way to remember where you are as you work across the row. You can create a chart like the one shown below to tell you where you are on each section for any given row.

Row number	4 Row Pattern	6 Row Pattern	8 Row Pattern	12 Row Pattern
1	1	1	1	1
	2	2	2	2
	3	3	3	3
	4	4	4	4
	1	5	5	5
	2	6	6	6
	3	1	7	7
	4	2	8	8
	1	3	1	9
	2	4	2	10
	3	5	3	11
	4	6	4	12
	1	1	5	1
	2	2	6	2

Things to watch for when designing with cables:

- A simple cable up the center front of a sweater can turn a plain garment into a dynamic one that is more interesting to knit. It doesn't take a lot of cables to make a garment look spectacular.

- Cables tend to pull the knitting in, or tighten up the stitch gauge. The stitch gauge over a cable pattern will be much tighter than the stitch gauge over a stockinette section of knitting. If you are going to use multiple cables across a piece of knitting, a stitch gauge must be made for each one. A sweater front with 100 stitches in plain stockinette stitch might need 120 stitches to equal the same width if a large cable is used up the front.

Generally if multiple cables are worked across the entire width of the piece, they are separated by sections of reverse stockinette or moss stitch. Cables are usually made up of knit stitches, while purl stitches are used to form the background. The knit stitches stand out against the purl stitch background. There is no reason why stockinette stitch cables can't be placed on a stockinette stitch background. They might disappear a little, but that might be the desired look.

Another option is stockinette stitch cables on a garter stitch background as seen in the Cabled Stole. The garter stitch for the borders and shawl collar of the stole is repeated between the cables, giving the stole an interesting look without making it difficult to knit. The cable in the stole is a simple one on which to learn. It is a simple six-stitch cable that gets "turned" every eighth row.

The Cabled Scarf is a bit more challenging because it includes cables that are turned on every other row, as well as a very interesting cable that requires two cable needles. I used this pattern because it demonstrates the different ways cables can be made and because it is in a ribbing pattern that lends itself well to a scarf. It does not require borders to keep it flat and, unlike most cable patterns, it has a wrong side attractive enough that if the scarf gets turned over it doesn't look inside out. The scarf is knit in a lighter weight yarn than the stole, which makes it drape nicely around the neck. The lighter weight yarn also keeps the scarf from getting too thick, which heavily cabled patterns tend to do.

Both of the patterns are charted because writing the patterns in charts is simpler than writing row-by-row instructions. As described in the comments about reading charts (see page 7), the charts give a picture of what is happening in both of the designs. Both right and wrong side rows are charted in the patterns. The symbols used in the charts are explained in the directions given with both charts. A diagonal line represents the direction the cable is being moved or twisted.

CABLED STOLE

MATERIALS

4 skeins of Wensleydale Longwool from
   Berroco (100% wool, 174yds/100g); color
   115 Damask
Size 9 US (5.5mm) circular needles (29")
Size 10 US (6mm) knitting needles, or size
   required to obtain gauge

Gauge: 16 sts and 24 rows = 4" in garter
   stitch on larger needles

DIRECTIONS

NOTE: *All rows are charted.*

With size 9 circular needles, CO 27 sts, K 7 rows.
Change to size 10 needles and begin chart.
Work to row 144. Work rows A through H twice.
   If you wish to make the shawl longer, work
   more repeats of rows A through H.
Work rows 144 to row 1, working a decrease
   instead of an increase where designated on
   chart.
Change to size 9 circular needles, K 7 rows. BO
   loosely.

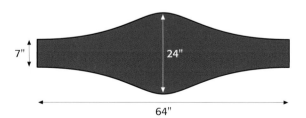

Border on Lower Edge

With RS facing, use size 9 circular needles to pick
up and K1 st in each garter stitch knot and 2 sts
out of every 3 rows in stockinette sections along
outside edge of shawl. K 7 rows. BO loosely.

FINISHING

Weave in all ends. Steam gently.

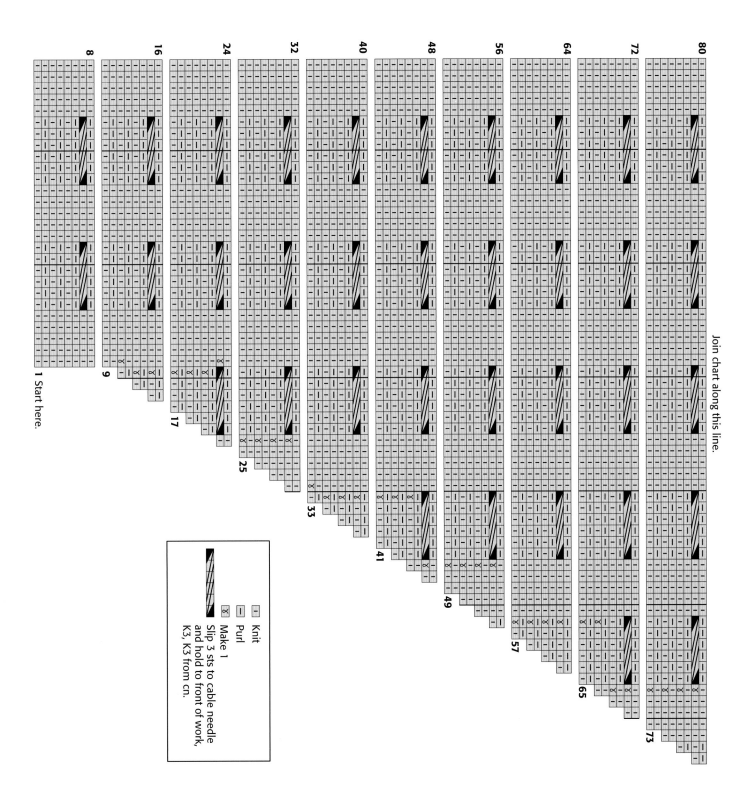

Join chart along this line.

Knit

Purl

Make 1

Slip 3 sts to cable needle
and hold to front of work,
K3, K3 from cn.

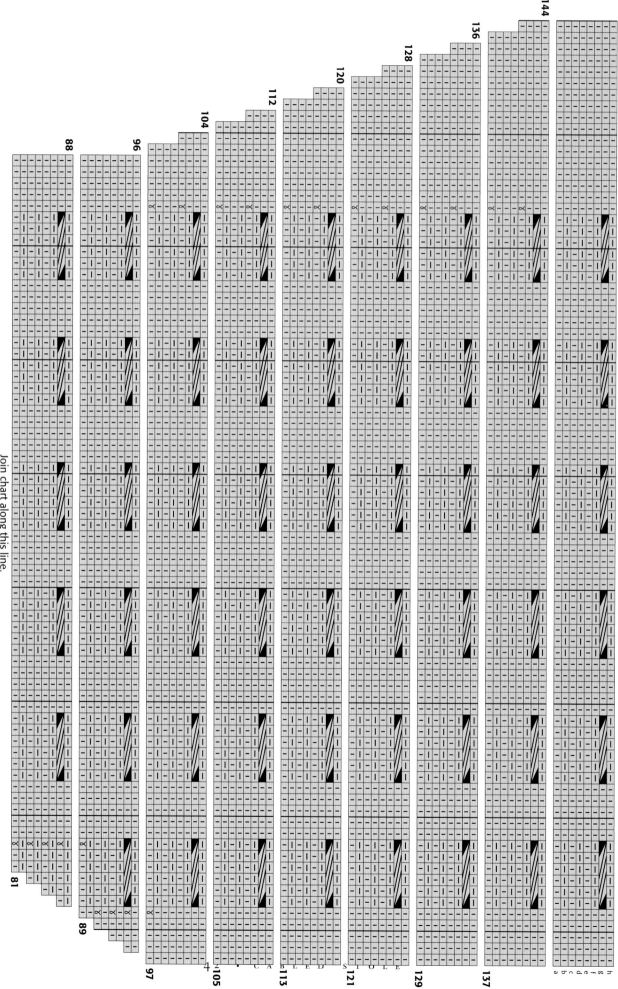

Join chart along this line.

CABLED SCARF

MATERIALS

3 skeins of Creme Brulee, DK by Knit One,
   Crochet Too (100% superwash wool,
   131yds/50g); color 420
Size 6 US (4.25mm) knitting needles, or size
   required to obtain gauge

Gauge: 26 sts and 30 rows = 4", in K2, P2 ribbing with sample slightly stretched

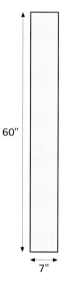

DIRECTIONS

NOTE: *All rows are charted.*

CO 54 sts loosely. Work rows 1 through 30 of
chart 12 times. Work rows 1 and 2. BO loosely.

FINISHING

Weave in ends. Block.

Chart columns numbered across the top: 29, 27, 25, 23, 21, 19, 17, 15, 13, 11, 9, 7, 5, 3, 1

Across the bottom: 30, 28, 26, 24, 22, 20, 18, 16, 14, 12, 10, 8, 6, 4, 2

Start here.

Legend:

● P on RS rows, K on WS rows

☐ K on RS rows, P on WS rows

sl 4 sts onto cable needle and hold to back, K2, sl last 2 sts from cable needle back onto left needle and P these 2 sts, then K2 from cable needle

sl 2 sts onto first cable needle and hold to front, sl 2 sts only to second cable needle and hold to back, K2, P2 from second cable needle, then K2 from first cable needle

sl 2 sts onto cable needle and hold to back, K2, K2 from cable needle

sl 2 sts onto cable needle and hold to front, K2, K2 from cable needle

sl 2 sts onto cable needle and hold to back, K2, P2 from cable needle

sl 2 sts onto cable needle and hold to front, P2, K2 from cable needle

SHORT ROWS

ORKING WITH SHORT rows is a very interesting way to add shape to a garment. It is absolutely magical to watch how short rows can form a heel or make a dart. For our purposes, short rows are used in shawls to make them fit around the body better and hang more attractively. Short rows can be placed in the back of the garment, as in the Charming Mohair Short Rows Stole. Or the entire shawl can be shaped with short rows as in the Gossamer Short Rows Shawl.

Short rows get their name because they are a shorter row. It means that the entire number of stitches on the needle are not being worked in one row. Let's say you have fifty stitches on the needle. The directions might tell you to knit twenty-five stitches, turn the work, and purl back. Hence, two shorter rows were made. The problem with turning knitting in the middle of the row is that it makes a hole. Holes might be acceptable in some work, as in a lace shawl, but for the most part they aren't. To close up the holes, you need to take a couple of steps while knitting. See "Basic Short Rows" on page 10 for detailed instructions. The following patterns tell you where to place these steps.

Designing with short rows can be a little tricky, but it is always interesting. Short rows make one side of the knitting "higher" or "taller" than the other side. So, if you work short rows on the knit side with the right side facing, the right side of the knitting will be higher than the left side of the knitting. Short rows worked on the purl side will make the left side of the knitting higher. The above is a basic description, but if you look at shawl shaping you can see why it is useful information. Short rows can be used for shoulder shaping in basically the same way.

On the Charming Mohair Short Rows Stole, the short rows are at the center back. The bottom area needs to be larger than the neck area. When you work short rows on the knit side, you create more rows of knitting at the bottom edge than at the neck edge. This makes the shawl wrap around the body nicely and eliminates extra fabric at the neck. On the Gossamer Short Rows Shawl, you repeat short rows around the shawl, creating a very large diameter at the bottom of the shawl in comparison to the diameter at the neck. The sections look like pieces of a pie.

CHARMING MOHAIR SHORT ROWS STOLE

MATERIALS

3 skeins of Kid Extrafine Mohair by Filanda
from Trendsetter Yarns (80% mohair, 20%
nylon, 250yds/25g); color 24

7 skeins of Charm by Trendsetter Yarns (77%
polyester, 23% polyamide Tactel,
95yds/20g); color 1480

1 skein of Sunshine by Trendsetter Yarns (75%
rayon, 25% nylon, 95yds/50g); color 48

Size 9 US (5.5mm) knitting needles or size
required to obtain gauge

Size G crochet hook

Gauge: 14 stitches and 20 rows = 4" in
stockinette stitch

DIRECTIONS

Holding a strand each of Mohair and Charm
together throughout, CO 8 sts. Work in stockinette stitch as follows: inc 1 st at the beginning of
every 4th row until there are 60 sts. Inc 1 st at the
beginning of every other row until there are 64
sts. Work 40 rows without shaping. NOTE: *All
increases and decreases are worked on knit rows.*

Begin shaping with short rows as follows:
Work to 4 sts from the end, W and T, P back.
Work to 8 sts from the end, W and T, P back.
Work to 12 sts from the end, W and T, P back.
Work to 16 sts from the end, W and T, P back.
Work to 20 sts from the end, W and T, P back.
Work to 24 sts from the end, W and T, P back.
Work to 28 sts from the end, W and T, P back.
Work to 32 sts from the end, W and T, P back.
Work to 36 sts from the end, W and T, P back.

Work to 40 sts from the end, W and T, P back.
Work to 44 sts from the end, W and T, P back.
Work to 48 sts from the end, W and T, P back.
Work to 52 sts from the end, W and T, P back.
Work to 56 sts from the end, W and T, P back.
Work to 60 sts from the end, W and T, P back. K
across, knitting up wraps. P 1 row. K4, W and T,
P back. (NOTE: *On all of the following knit rows
remember to knit up the wrap as you pass it from the
previous row.*) Work 8 sts, W and T, P back. Work
12 sts, W and T, P back. Work 16 sts, W and T, P
back. Work 20 sts, W and T, P back. Work 24 sts,
W and T, P back. Work 28 sts, W and T, P back.
Work 32sts, W and T, P back. Work 36 sts, W and
T, P back. Work 40 sts, W and T, P back. Work 44
sts, W and T, P back. Work 48 sts, W and T, P
back. Work 52 sts, W and T, P back. Work 56 sts,
W and T, P back. Work 60 sts, W and T, P back.
Work 42 rows without shaping. Dec 1 st at the
beginning of every other row until there are 60
sts. Dec 1 st at the beginning of every fourth row
until there are 8 sts. K 4 rows. BO.

FINISHING

Starting at center back neck with RS facing and
using Sunshine, work 1 single crochet into 2 out
of every 3 sts to point, 3 sts in corner, 6 sts across
point, 3 sts in corner, 1 st into 3 out of every 4
rows to other point, 3 sts in corner, 6 sts across
point, 3 sts in corner, 1 st into 2 out of every 3 sts,
end by joining with a slip stitch. Do not turn
work, work 1 row of backward single crochet into
each st around. Join with a slip stitch. Finish off.
Block with steam so all edges lie flat.

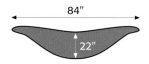

GOSSAMER SHORT ROWS SHAWL

MATERIALS

- 3 skeins of Gossamer by Karabella Yarns (30% Kid Mohair, 52% nylon, 18% polyester, 222yds/50g); color 6142
- Size 10 US (6mm) circular needle (24") or size required to obtain gauge
- Size 7 US (4.5mm) knitting needles for border or size required to obtain gauge
- Stainless steel T-pins for blocking

Gauge: 14 sts and 20 rows = 4" in stockinette stitch

DIRECTIONS

With size 10 needles, CO 81 sts. P 1 row.
Next row: (K2tog, YO) across, end K1.
Next row: P.
Next row: K1, YO, K2tog, K to last 3 sts, K2tog, YO, K1. Repeat last 2 rows once.

Begin shaping with short rows as follows:
*P 77 sts, W and T, K to last 3 sts, K2tog, YO, K1.
P73 sts, W and T, K to last 3 sts, K2tog, YO, K1.
P69 sts, W and T, K to last 3 sts, K2tog, YO, K1.
P65 sts, W and T, K to last 3 sts, K2tog, YO, K1.
P61 sts, W and T, K to last 3 sts, K2tog, YO, K1.
P57 sts, W and T, K to last 3 sts, K2tog, YO, K1.
P53 sts, W and T, K to last 3 sts, K2tog, YO, K1.
P49 sts, W and T, K to last 3 sts, K2tog, YO, K1.
P45 sts, W and T, K to last 3 sts, K2tog, YO, K1.
P41 sts, W and T, K to last 3 sts, K2tog, YO, K1.
P37 sts, W and T, K to last 3 sts, K2tog, YO, K1.
P33 sts, W and T, K to last 3 sts, K2tog, YO, K1.
P29 sts, W and T, K to last 3 sts, K2tog, YO, K1.
P25 sts, W and T, K to last 3 sts, K2tog, YO, K1.
P21 sts, W and T, K to last 3 sts, K2tog, YO, K1.

P17 sts, W and T, K to last 3 sts, K2tog, YO, K1.
P13 sts, W and T, K to last 3 sts, K2tog, YO, K1.
P9 sts, W and T, K to last 3 sts, K2tog, YO, K1.
P5, W and T, K to last 3 sts, K2tog, YO, K1. P 1 row, purling up wraps.** (Next row: K1, YO, K2tog, K to last 3 sts, K2tog, YO, K1. Next row: P across.) 4 times. Next row: K1, YO, K2tog, K to last 3 sts, K2tog, YO, K1.* Repeat from * to * 7 times. Repeat from * to ** once. Next row: K1, YO, K2tog, K to last 3 sts, K2tog, YO, K1. Next row: P across. Repeat last 2 rows once. Next row: (K2tog, YO) across, end K1. Next row: P. BO loosely.

Border pattern
With size 7 needles, CO 6 sts.
Rows 1, 3, 5, and 7: Sl 1 wyib, K1, YO, SSK, YO, K to end.
Rows 2, 4, and 6: K to last 3 sts, YO, SSK, sl 1, pick up 1 st in YO of shawl, psso.
Row 8: Use partial-row bind-off to BO 4 sts, K2, YO, SSK, sl 1, pick up 1 st in YO of shawl, psso.
Repeat around shawl using the following formula: Start at left front neck edge with RS facing. Use each YO on front edge twice. Work 8 rows of border in last YO at bottom corner. Use each YO along bottom edge once, then work 8 rows of border in last YO at bottom corner. Use each YO on front edge and around neck twice. End with row 8. Graft end of border to CO sts at beginning of border.

FINISHING

Weave in all ends. Moisten. Pin shawl to shape using T-pins. Pin out each point of the border.

LACE

OFTEN THOUGHT TO be the premier knitting technique, lace is really some of the simplest knitting you can do. Of course, some patterns are more difficult than others, but if you can follow directions accurately, lace can be accomplished with very little difficulty. Lace patterns can actually be faster to knit than some other patterns. As you watch the shapes and patterns take place, the knitting is enjoyable, and you can't wait to see what is going to happen next. You can count on one thing about lace: no matter how simple or complicated a pattern, the result is always impressive.

With fine needles and thread, lace knitting has been used quite nicely to create wonderful borders for doilies or tablecloths. Knitted doilies are especially interesting to knit. Personally, I love knitting doilies just for the challenge.

You shape knitted lace with the type of decrease you use and where you place a yarn over in relationship to the decrease. Decreases can slant either to the right or the left. When you place them in certain combinations, one type of decrease will counteract the other type of decrease and the knitting will remain vertical and horizontal. Remember the Chenille Diagonal Lace Scarf (page 20), in which the decreases were used purposely to create the shape?

Large shawls made of lace in very fine yarn, such as the Shetland Island shawls, must be stretched out and allowed to dry, a process known in the Shetland Islands as "dressing." In the United States we refer to the dampening, stretch-ing, and/or steaming of a garment or piece of lace as "blocking." Knitted lace generally needs quite a bit of blocking to open up the yarn overs and make the lace look its lacy best. Until a piece is blocked, it often has a "dishrag" look to it. Don't worry; the blocking will turn it into the wonderful, gossamer-looking piece it is meant to be. Unfortunately, blocking also may reveal mistakes if you have not watched the rows and stitch numbers carefully while knitting.

There are various terms and symbols used to describe the steps in knitting lace. If a chart is provided for a lace pattern, the symbols are defined next to the chart. These symbols may vary from chart to chart, even within the same pattern book. When I wrote the book *Lace from the Attic, a Victorian Notebook of Knitted Laces*, I researched lace patterns and abbreviations used by different people to knit lace. It was fascinating to discover that so many differences existed from knitter to knitter and from era to era, all to produce the same type of knitting.

Lace patterns can be knit in yarns of various weights and sizes. The Lace Scarf is a good example of lace knit on medium-size needles using two fine yarns held together to create a medium-weight yarn. The equally beautiful Wigwam Shawl, on the other hand, was knit on big needles using a ribbon-type yarn.

The Lace Scarf presented here starts in an unusual manner. Rather than starting at one end of the scarf and knitting to the other end, use a provisional cast on instead of a regular cast on to start in the middle or back neck. When one side is completed, remove the provisional cast on, pick up stitches, and then repeat the pattern for the other side of the scarf. Repeat the simple leaf pattern over and over until you have achieved the desired length. Then shape the points. This method creates a seamless scarf.

The Wigwam Shawl, on the other hand, starts at the neck and is knit toward the bottom instead of starting at the bottom and working toward the neck, the more usual progression. Decreases and yarn overs are used as they normally are in lace (that is, for every decrease there is a yarn over), except at center back, where there are yarn overs not associated with a decrease. It is these yarn overs (or increases) that make the shawl bigger as it is worked.

The Shoulder Warmer Shawl represents yet another way to approach knitting a shawl. It starts at the point of the back and works toward the shoulders using yarn overs for the increases and extending the pattern into the extra stitches. At the shoulder/neck area, the piece is divided, a back neck is made, and the left and right shoulder areas are knit separately and finished off. There are no seams in this design either. The basic lace pattern used for the shawl is done in garter stitch. If you prefer a stockinette stitch for the background, simply purl back before and after the lace border. Leave the borders in garter stitch to keep the edges flat. The shawl could be knit in various fibers, including cotton or silk, for a different look. Changing the needle size to accommodate the different fibers would also change the size of the shawl.

Finally, the Lavender Linen Lace Shawl is a basic triangle started at the point and worked toward the larger end. Its beautiful lace pattern incorporates yarn overs for the increases, which also become part of the pattern. This pattern may look difficult, but it is a good example of a lace pattern that is repetitive, builds on itself, and is easy to memorize and work. It is interesting to watch the progression as one set of leaves ends and another set begins. The linen in this shawl is a wonderful weight for wearing in the summer. The crispness of the yarn gives a very distinct look to the leaves. You could knit the shawl in wool or any other fiber, changing its look completely. A warm, fall-colored yarn like gold or persimmon would give the leaves more an autumn than a spring look.

LACE SCARF

MATERIALS

3 skeins of Richesse et Soie by Knit One,
Crochet Too (65% cashmere, 35% silk,
145yds/25g); color 9243

2 skeins of Douceur et Soie by Knit One,
Crochet Too (70% baby mohair, 30% silk,
225yds/25g); color 8248

3 yards waste yarn for provisional cast on

Crochet hook, size G

Size 8 US (5mm) knitting needles, or size
required to obtain gauge

Gauge: 18 sts and 24 rows = 4" in stockinette
stitch

DIRECTIONS

NOTE: *Only right-side rows are charted. All wrong-side rows: K5, P to last 5 sts, K5.*

Using both yarns held together throughout, CO 33 sts using provisional cast on (see page 8). K5, P23, K5. Begin chart.

Work rows 1 through 16 once, then rows 17 through 30 nine times or for desired length. Finish chart.

Remove provisional cast on, place sts on needle, and repeat chart as above.

FINISHING

Weave in all ends. Rinse out, roll in a towel, pin out, and lay flat to dry.

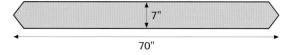

7"

70"

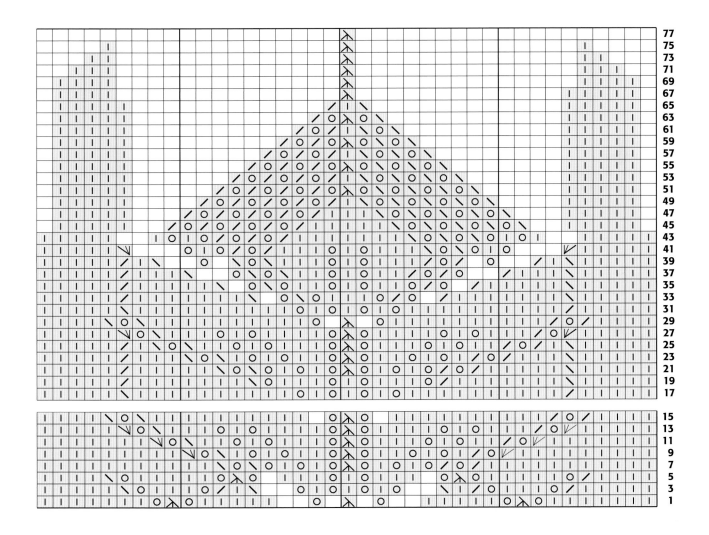

Knit — I

YO — O

SSK — \

K2tog — /

CC Dec (sl2, K1, p2sso) — ⟍ (with line)

K3tog — ⟋ (with line)

sl1, K2tog, psso — ⟋⟍

All even-numbered (WS) rows: K5, P to last 5 sts, K5

You can make this shawl larger by casting on more stitches in multiples of 4 and increasing the number of repeats of the pattern before and after the center by 1 for each 4 stitches added.

FINISHED DIMENSIONS: 30" X 51" AFTER BLOCKING

MATERIALS

5 skeins of Hand Dyed Wigwam by Colinette Yarn, Ltd. (100% cotton, 187yds/100g); color 101, Monet

Size 10½ US (6.5mm) knitting needles, or size required to obtain gauge

Stainless steel T-pins for blocking

Gauge: 16 sts and 24 rows = 4" in garter stitch

DIRECTIONS

NOTE: *Slip first stitch at beginning of every row as if to purl with yarn in front.*

CO 63 sts, K 9 rows.

Row 1: Sl 1, K4, (YO, K2tog) 13 times, YO, K1, YO, (SSK, YO) 13 times, K5; 65 sts.

Row 2 and all wrong side rows: Sl 1, K4, P to last 5 sts, K5.

Row 3: Sl 1, K4, (YO, K2tog) 13 times, (YO, K1) 3 times, YO, (SSK, YO) 13 times, K5; 69 sts.

Row 5. Sl 1, K4, (YO, K2tog) 14 times, (YO, K1) 3 times, YO, (SSK, YO) 14 times, K5; 73 sts.

Row 7: Sl 1, K4, (YO, K2tog) 15 times, (YO, K1) 3 times, YO, (SSK, YO) 15 times, K5; 77 sts.

Row 9: Sl 1, K4, (YO, K2tog) 16 times, (YO, K1) 3 times, YO, (SSK, YO) 16 times, K5; 81 sts.

Continue working in this manner until back measures 25" down center back. End with odd-numbered row. Next row: Sl 1 st, K across. Next row: Work pattern as established. Next row: BO loosely.

FINISHING

Weave in all ends. Moisten and block to finished measurement with T-pins.

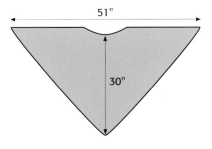

SHOULDER WARMER SHAWL

MATERIALS

2 skeins of GGH Mohair 3000 (70% mohair,
   20% wool, 10% nylon, 165yds/50g);
   color 34
Size 10 US (6mm) knitting needles, or size
   required to obtain gauge
2 stitch markers
Stainless steel T-pins for blocking

Gauge: 14 sts and 24 rows = 4" in garter
   stitch

Please read before beginning your shawl:

- Use stitch markers to designate the edge stitches.

- Instead of knitting each stitch at the shoulder stitches as indicated on the chart, you can slip the first stitch. This creates a very nice edge that looks like an elongated knit stitch. To do this, work chart B and chart C as follows: On the inside neck section only, slip the first stitch at the beginning of the row as if to purl with the yarn in front, move the yarn to the knit position, and continue with the chart. On chart C, slip the stitch at the beginning of the wrong side row, and on chart B, slip the stitch on the beginning of the right side row. If you slip the first stitch on the inside edge, that counts as a stitch on the chart.

DIRECTIONS

NOTE: *Only right-side rows are charted. Knit all wrong-side rows.*

CO 4 sts.
Row 1: K4.
Row 2: K2, YO, K2; 5sts.
Row 3: K2 YO, K1, YO, K2; 7 sts.
Row 4: K2, YO, K3, YO, K2; 9 sts.
Row 5: K9
Row 6: K2, YO, K2tog, K1, SSK YO, K2; 9 sts.
Row 7: K9

Go to chart A. When chart A is completed, continue with chart B. When chart B is completed, continue with chart C. Finish off. Weave in the ends.

FINISHING

Rinse in warm water, roll in a towel, and squeeze gently. Lay on a flat surface and pin out each point. Do not remove pins until dry.

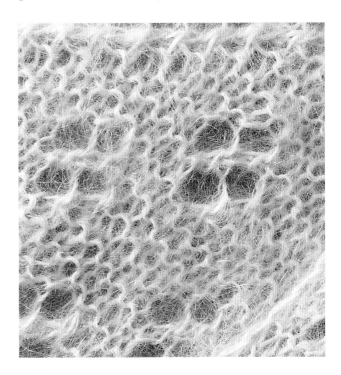

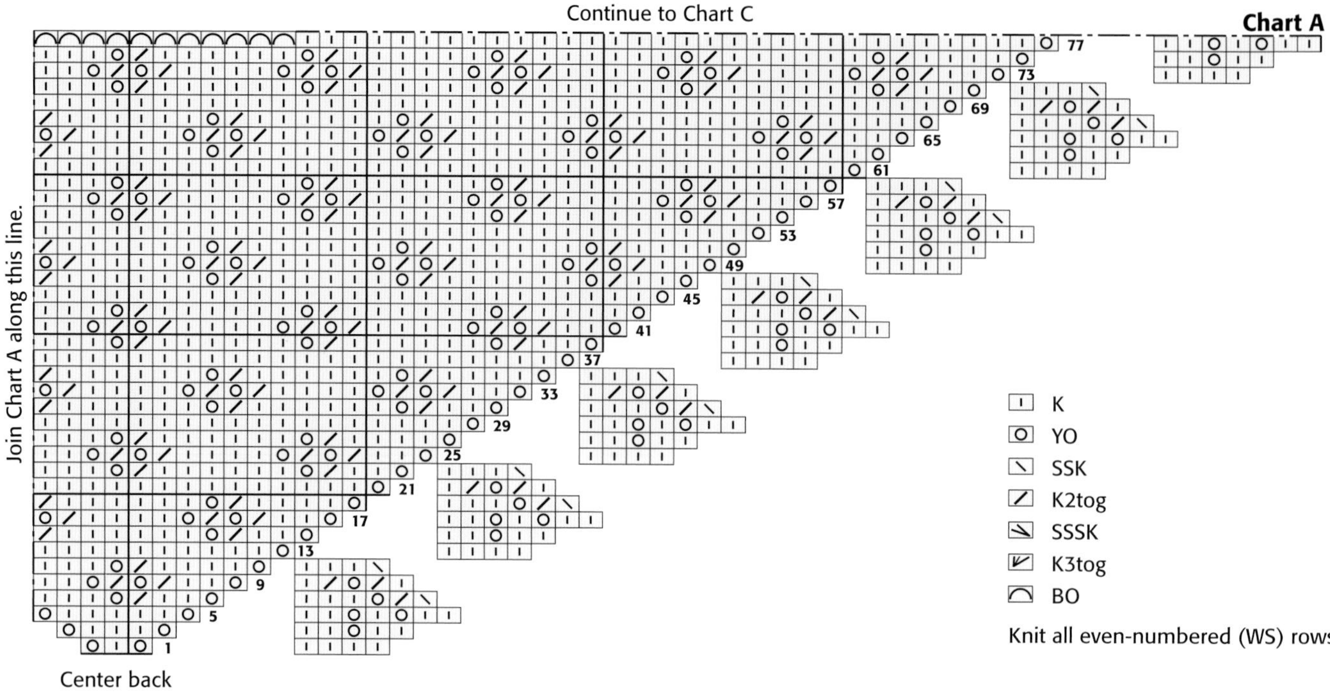
Continue to Chart C
Chart A
Join Chart A along this line.
Center back
1
5
9
13
17
21
25
29
33
37
41
45
49
53
57
61
65
69
73
77

K
YO
SSK
K2tog
SSSK
K3tog
BO

Knit all even-numbered (WS) rows.

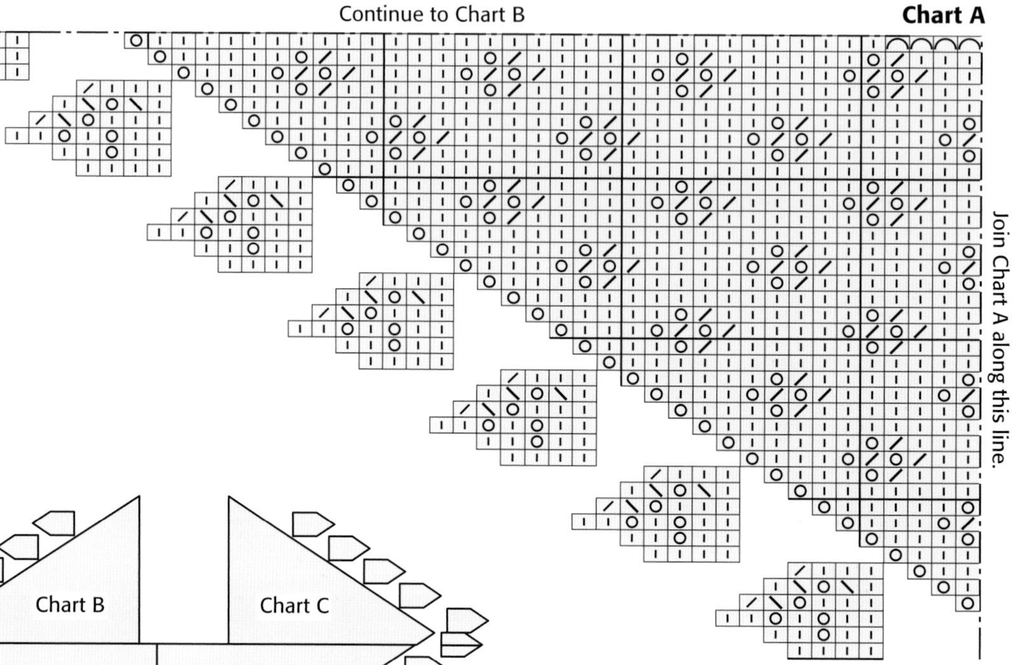
Continue to Chart B
Chart A
Join Chart A along this line.

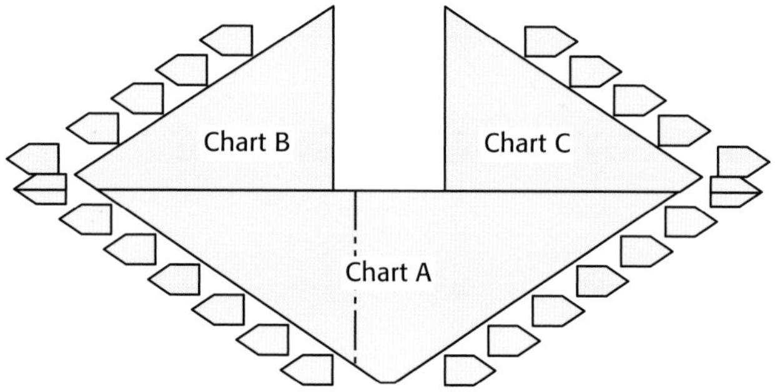
Chart B
Chart C
Chart A

Legend

- ⊡ K
- ⊙ YO
- ◿ SSK
- ◺ K2tog
- ◥ SSSK
- ◪ K3tog
- ⌒ BO

Knit all even-numbered (WS) rows.

Chart B

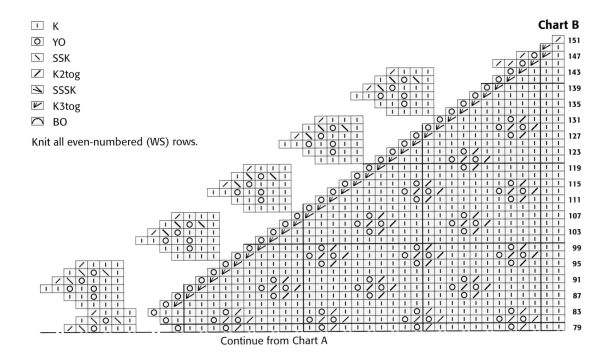

151
147
143
139
135
131
127
123
119
115
111
107
103
99
95
91
87
83
79

Continue from Chart A

Chart C

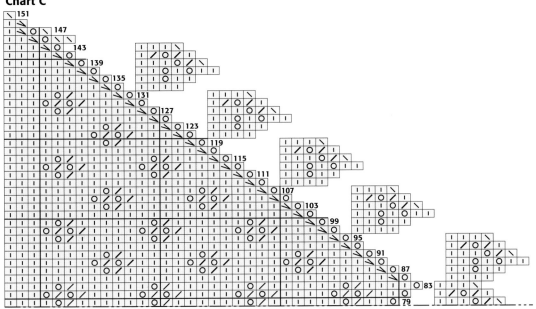

151
147
143
139
135
131
127
123
119
115
111
107
103
99
95
91
87
83
79

Continue from Chart A

LAVENDER LINEN LACE SHAWL

MATERIALS

8 oz of Euroflax Linen from Louet Sales (100% linen, 1300yds/pound); color Grape

Size 4 US (3.5mm) circular needles (29"), or size required to obtain gauge

Stainless steel T-pins for blocking

Gauge: 20 sts and 28 rows = 4" in stockinette stitch

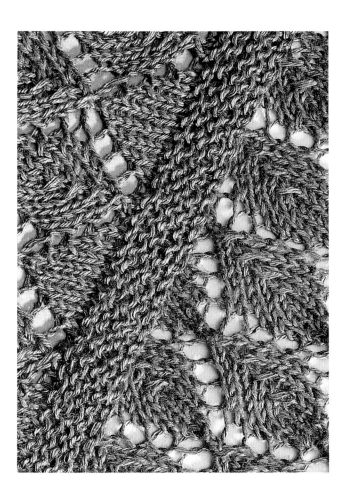

DIRECTIONS

NOTE: *All rows are charted.*

Sl 1 st at beg of every row as if to P wyif. This counts as 1 stitch on the chart.

Follow chart, repeating rows 31 through 46 eleven times. Repeat the center section as the shawl enlarges. The charts for the edge sections will remain the same throughout. The pattern may be continued if you desire a larger shawl. End with row 46. K 9 rows. BO loosely.

FINISHING

Immerse shawl in cool water, rinse out, and roll in a towel to absorb excess moisture. Pin out on flat surface. Do not remove until dry.

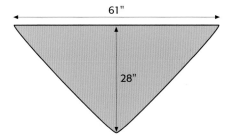

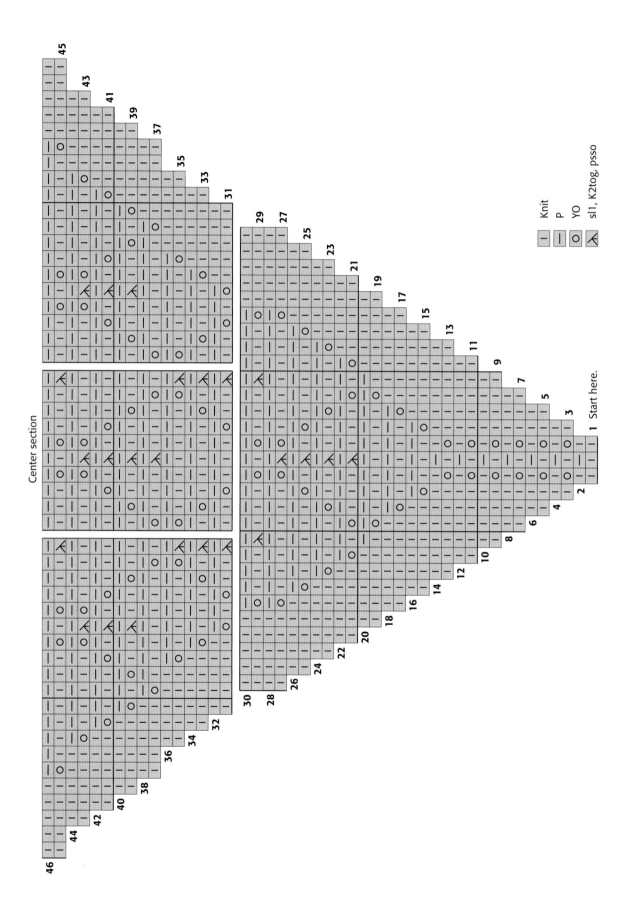

Center section

Knit
P
YO
sl1, K2tog, psso

GARTER STITCH SQUARES

INTERLOCKING SQUARES AND diamonds are represented in three different techniques. In order of increasing difficulty, they are garter stitch squares, interlocking diamonds (page 70), and entrelac (page 75). All of the shapes are wonderful to work with if you want to create a specific color pattern or use novelty or variegated yarns. The key elements that differ in the techniques are the decrease and stitch patterns used and the way the stitches are picked up. Garter stitch squares are knit in garter stitch because it is the "squarest" stitch we have. The squares start out as a straight piece of knitting, but a decrease up the center "miters" the stitches into a square. If you used stockinette stitch for the mitered squares, they wouldn't be square; they would be more of a rectangle, or a diamond if placed on-point. Then you would have an interlocking diamond.

The basic pattern for the squares, including the decrease used to miter each square, is as follows: Cast on an odd number of stitches. Knit 1 row. Work to the center 3 stitches, slip 1 stitch, knit 2 stitches together, and then pass the slipped stitch over. Repeat these 2 rows until there is 1 stitch left. Finish off. This creates a nice diagonal line up the center of the square. It slants either right or left depending on how you cast on or pick up the stitches and how you hold the square for the next step.

To start the first square, you must cast on the total number of stitches used for the square and work the basic pattern. If you hold the square one way, it will have a right-slanting diagonal line up

its center. If you hold it another way, the diagonal line will slant to the left. In our case, we want the line to slant left.

All stitches cast on

Holding the square so the tail from finishing is in the upper left corner, pick up 11 stitches down the left edge of the square just finished and cast on 10 stitches using the cable cast on. Work these 21 stitches to make the next square. Repeat to add one more square, completing the first row and the bottom of the scarf.

Make more squares by following the diagram for the scarf, using the following rules.

- If squares are being worked to create an edge, the "edge" parts of the squares are made of cast on stitches (see blue lines on the diagram).

Starting here

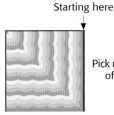

Pick up stitches along edge of adjoining square.

Cast on remaining stitches.

- Squares may be made of any combination of cast on stitches and picked up stitches.

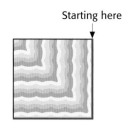

Remainder of stitches cast on

← Starting here

Stitches picked up along edge of adjoining square

- If squares are being worked where both edges already exist from previous squares, stitches are all picked up (see red lines on drawing).

Starting here ↓

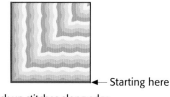

All stitches are picked up.

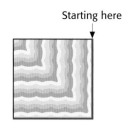

← Starting here

Pick up stitches along edge of adjoining square.

- Squares of varying sizes can be joined together. Use multiples of the stitch numbers that created the original squares minus one. Example: Two twenty-one-stitch squares on top of each other can have a forty-one-stitch square placed beside them.

21-stitch squares   41-stitch square

The diagram of the Garter Stitch Squares Scarf on page 69 illustrates how a series of twenty-one-stitch and forty-one-stitch squares are used in alternating colors to create a wonderful series of squares with diagonal lines slanting to the right or the left. The diagram will assist you in learning the different ways of forming each square. Once you have learned the techniques, you can create your own design. All the diagonal lines could slant the same direction, or they could change, as they do in the Garter Stitch Squares Scarf. A simple vest might look like this.

The math involved in creating this garment is rather simple: If you need a size 40" vest, and there are ten squares across the bottom of the garment, then each square has to measure 4" (10 x 4" = 40"). All of the shaping involved in creating necks and armholes is done by simply leaving out squares. I like to use ten squares as the basis for the design because it is such an easy number to work with when shaping and adjusting the size of the garment. Twelve or twenty would also work, depending on the size squares you want to make. Using the size 40" vest as an example again: if you wanted the design to have twenty squares instead of ten, you would need twenty 2" squares across the bottom.

Garter Stitch Squares Scarf

MATERIALS

3 skeins each of color 4333 (Color A) and
color 4555 (Color B), Parfait Swirls by
Knit One, Crochet Too (100 % wool,
100yds/50g)

Size 8 US (5mm) knitting needles, or size
required to obtain gauge

Gauge: One 21-stitch square = 2½"

Small square worked over 21 sts.
Row 1 and all odd rows: K across.
Row 2: K9, sl 1, K2tog, psso, K9.
Row 4: K8, sl 1, K2tog, psso, K8.
Row 6: K7, sl 1, K2tog, psso, K7.
Row 8: K6, sl 1, K2tog, psso, K6.
Row 10: K5, sl 1, K2tog, psso, K5.
Row 12: K4, sl 1, K2tog, psso, K4.
Row 14: K3, sl 1, K2tog, psso, K3.
Row 16: K2, sl 1, K2tog, psso, K2.
Row 18: K1, sl 1, K2tog, psso, K1.
Row 20: Sl 1, K2tog, psso. Finish off.

Large square worked over 41 sts.
Row 1 and all odd rows: K across.
Row 2: K19, sl 1, K2tog, psso, K19.
Row 4: K18, sl 1, K2tog, psso, K18.
Row 6: K17, sl 1, K2tog, psso, K17.
Row 8: K16, sl 1, K2tog, psso, K16.
Row 10: K15, sl 1, K2tog, psso, K15.
Row 12: K14, sl 1, K2tog, psso, K14.
Row 14: K13, sl 1, K2tog, psso, K13.
Row 16: K12, sl 1, K2tog, psso, K12.
Row 18: K11, sl 1, K2tog, psso, K11.
Row 20: K10, sl 1, K2tog, psso, K10.
Row 22: K9, sl 1, K2tog, psso, K9.
Row 24: K8, sl 1, K2tog, psso, K8.

Row 26: K7, sl 1, K2tog, psso, K7.
Row 28: K6, sl 1, K2tog, psso, K6.
Row 30: K5, sl 1, K2tog, psso, K5.
Row 32: K4, sl 1, K2tog, psso, K4.
Row 34: K3, sl 1, K2tog, psso, K3.
Row 36: K2, sl 1, K2tog, psso, K2.
Row 38: K1, sl 1, K2tog, psso, K1.
Row 40: Sl 1, K2tog, psso. Finish off.

DIRECTIONS

NOTE: *Use cabled CO whenever casting on after picking up sts.*

Following the diagram on page 69, proceed as follows:

Square 1: Using color A, CO 21 sts. Work small square pattern.

Square 2: Turn square 1 so diagonal line is to left. Using color B, pick up 11 sts along left edge. CO 10 sts using cabled CO. Work small square.

Square 3: Using color B, pick up 11 sts along left edge of square 2. CO 10 sts using cabled CO. Work small square.

Square 4: Using color B, pick up 11 sts across top of square 3. CO 10 sts. Work small square.

Square 5: Using color A, pick up 11 sts across top of square 4. CO 10 sts. Work small square.

Square 6: Using color B, pick up 20 sts across top of squares 1 and 2, 1 st in the corner of square 3, 20 sts up edge of squares 4 and 5. Work large square.

Square 7: Using color B, CO 11 sts. Pick up 10 sts across one half of top of square 6. Work small square.

Square 8: Using color A, pick up 10 sts down left side of square 7, 1 st in corner, 10 sts across remaining half of square 6. Work small square.

Square 9: Using color B, pick up 10 sts down left side of square 8, 1 st in corner, 10 sts across top of square 5. Work small square.

Square 10: Using color A, CO 11 sts. Pick up 10 sts across top of square 7. Work small square.

Square 11: Using color B, CO 11 sts. Pick up 10 sts across top of square 10. Work small square.

Square 12: Using color A, pick up 20 sts down left side of squares 11 and 10, 1 st in corner and 20 more sts across top of squares 8 and 9. Work large square pattern.

Repeat squares 1 through 12 twice more, picking up sts instead of casting on sts for squares 1, 2, and 3. Work squares 1 through 9 once.

Side borders

On right-hand side of scarf and with RS of long edge facing, using color A, pick up and K10 sts on edges of small squares and 20 sts on edges of large squares. K 2 rows. BO loosely. Repeat on long edge of left-hand side with color B.

Bottom and top borders

On bottom edge, using color A, pick up and K2 sts in side border, 10 sts across each small square, and 2 sts in side border. K 2 rows. BO loosely. Repeat for top edge using color B.

FINISHING

Weave in all ends. Steam gently if necessary.

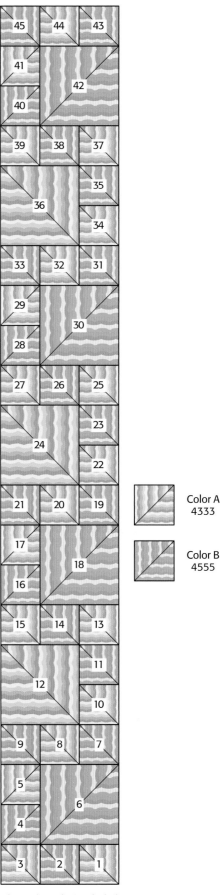

This diagram shows the order in which the squares are knit and the color used to knit them. Diagonal line shows the direction of decreases.

INTERLOCKING DIAMONDS

INTERLOCKING DIAMONDS ARE based on the same premise as garter stitch squares, but they are quite different. The decrease is slightly different, they are placed on-point, and they have diagonal edges instead of straight edges. In this book they are knit in stockinette stitch, but there is no reason why the diamond couldn't be created in seed stitch, lace, or other stitch patterns. You could change yarn colors halfway through the diamond or work in stripes. The possibilities are endless.

Each diamond is knit separately and joined to the diamond to the right and left of it when the stitches are picked up to begin the new diamond. The decrease for the diamonds is known as a *central chain decrease* and is noted with italics in the following instructions: Knit to the center 3 stitches, *slip 2 stitches together as if to knit, knit 1, pass the 2 slipped stitches over.* Purl the return row. Repeat these 2 rows until there are 3 stitches remaining,

work central chain decrease, do not purl back, place the last stitch on a pin. You use a pin instead of finishing off the stitch because you will use the stitch for the diamond you create above it.

Every diamond is knit in the same manner regardless of the number of stitches used to start it. Unlike garter stitch squares, interlocking diamonds have no straight edges, so you have to create half diamonds to make the side edges straight.

The Interlocking Diamonds Scarf was worked in two halves so that the diamonds at the ends would face the same direction when the scarf was draped around the neck. If it were knit all in one piece, the diamonds on one end would be upside down compared to the diamonds at the other end. The two halves are woven together at the back neck with a mattress stitch to create an invisible seam. I didn't need to work the Garter Stitch Squares Scarf in two halves because the squares look the same whether upside down or right side up.

MATERIALS

1 skein each of Alice Starmore Scottish
Campion (100% pure Shetland wool,
150yds/1oz) in the following colors: 235
Grouse for border, 587 Madder, 198
Copper, 1100 Autumn, 292 Pine Forest,
791 Oasis, 231 Bracken, 1190 Bronze

Size 4 US (3.5mm) knitting needles, or size
required to obtain gauge

Size 4 US (3.5mm) circular needles (29"), or
size required to obtain gauge, for side
borders

Small safety pins

Gauge: One diamond = 3" across widest point

ABBREVIATIONS USED

M 1: Make one by picking up yarn between
last stitch knit and next stitch on left needle and
knit into the back of it.

CC Dec: Slip 2 stitches together as if to knit,
knit 1, and pass 2 slipped stitches over.

DIRECTIONS

CO 69 sts using Color 235. K across.

Row 1: K2, M 1, (K9, work CC Dec, K9, M 1, K1,
M 1) across, end with K9, M 1, K2.

Row 2: K12, P1, (K10, P1) across, end with K12.
(Repeat rows 1 and 2) 4 times.

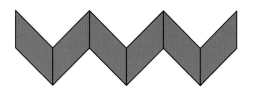

Beginning diamond

Place first 2 sts on a pin. Work on the next 21 sts
as follows:

**K9, work CC Dec, K9. Turn, P across.
Turn, *K8, work CC Dec, K8. Turn, P back.*
Repeat from * to * working 1 less stitch before and
after decrease. Place last stitch on pin. Cut yarn.**
Place next stitch on a pin. Repeat as above twice
for 2 more diamonds. You should have 3 diamonds
across the bottom. Place last 2 sts on a pin.

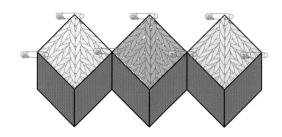

Right edge half diamond

With RS facing, remove safety pin and place 2 sts
on left knitting needle. Using appropriate color, K
the 2 sts. Pick up 10 sts up edge of first diamond.
*Turn, P across. Turn, K1, SSK, K to end. *
Repeat from * to * until 2 sts remain. Place last 2
stitches on pin. Cut yarn.

Main diamond pattern

Stitch on safety pin from previous diamond

With RS facing, and starting one st below pin at top of a diamond, pick up and K10 sts down side of diamond. K1 st on pin (you can leave the pin and remove it when you have finished the diamond or remove it now if it gets in the way), pick up and K10 sts up side of adjoining diamond; 21 sts. Turn, P across. Work as for beginning diamond from ** to **. Repeat for one more diamond.

Left edge half diamond

With RS facing, pick up and K10 sts on left edge of last diamond in first row. K2 sts on pin. *Turn, P across. Turn, K to last 3 sts, K2 tog, K1.* Repeat from * to * until 2 sts remain. Place 2 sts on pin.

The scarf should now look like this.

The next row will consist of 3 main diamonds as shown below.

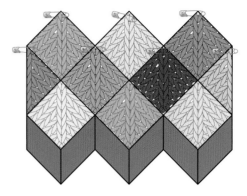

Following the diagram on page 74, continue to work diamonds and half diamonds, filling in the appropriate shapes. For a longer scarf, work in more diamonds and half diamonds on each half.

Work 4 small diamonds in place of 1 large diamond as follows:

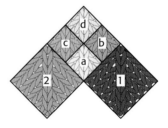

Small diamond A

At the appropriate space between 2 large diamonds, starting halfway down the left edge of diamond 1, pick up and K5 sts. K1 st on pin. Pick up 5 more sts up right side of adjoining diamond 2. *Turn, P across. Turn, K4, work CC Dec, K4.* Repeat from * to *, working one less st before and after dec as in main diamond. Place last st on pin.

Small diamond B

Starting 1 st below pin on left side of diamond 1, pick up and K5 sts. Pick up 1 st at join between diamond 1 and diamond A. Pick up and K5 more sts up right edge of diamond A. Repeat from * to * of small diamond A directions. Finish off.

Small diamond C

Starting 1 st below pin on left side of diamond A, pick up and K5 sts. Pick up 1 st at join between diamond 2 and diamond A. Pick up and K5 more sts up right edge of diamond 2. Repeat from * to * of small diamond A directions. Finish off.

Small diamond D

Starting 1 st below pin on left side of diamond B, pick up and K5 sts. K1 st on pin. Pick up and K5 more sts up right edge of diamond C. Repeat from * to * of small diamond A directions. Place last st on pin.

When first side is completed, finish off all diamonds and remove all pins.

Make second side following diagram for second half, beginning with border as for first side. When second side is completed, finish off all diamonds and remove all pins.

When 2 pieces are completed, fit the diamonds together and weave the seam together with a mattress stitch.

Side borders

With RS facing and starting at lower corner of border, use color 235 and a 29" needle to pick up and K5 sts in border, 10 sts on edge of each half diamond, and 5 sts in border. K 9 rows. BO loosely. Repeat for other side.

FINISHING

Weave in all ends. Gently rinse scarf to soften yarn. Lay flat to dry. Gently steam if necessary; do not flatten diamonds.

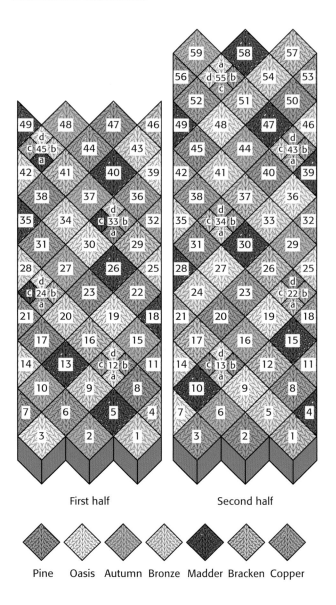

First half   Second half

Pine   Oasis   Autumn   Bronze   Madder   Bracken   Copper

ENTRELAC

THIS IS ONE of the most interesting techniques knitters can use to create wonderful texture and pattern in a design. The finished item can be made to look like basket weave if two colors are used, or can display a potpourri of textured patterns in each rectangle. Entrelac is composed of rectangles and triangles that, unlike the shapes in garter stitch squares or interlocking diamonds, are knit on the diagonal.

The entire process of entrelac is based on a series of picked-up stitches joined to the stitches of a square from a previous row. All stitches are on the needle at the same time, but only some of the stitches are knit or purled at a time. By contrast, in garter stitch squares and interlocking diamonds only the stitches of a specific motif are on the knitting needle at one time, and they eventually reduce down to one stitch.

As I describe the entrelac technique, I am tempted to say, "Trust me," numerous times. It seems a bit daunting when you look at the design and see the series of squares sitting at angles that take them off in different directions.

Here are some basic rules to think about when working entrelac:

- You knit only one rectangle or diamond at a time.

- You determine the width of the rectangle by the number of stitches picked up for each section.

- You determine the length of the rectangle by the number of rows worked, which is actually based on the number of stitches in the

rectangle to which the new rectangle is being joined.

- You use decreases to join the rectangles as they are being knit. Purl two together if joining on a purl row. Slip, slip, knit if joining on a knit row.

- You must work one whole row of rectangles, or rectangles and triangles, before the next row is started.

Generally, you start working entrelac by casting on the total number of stitches. Then you work base triangles to create a straight bottom edge. In the case of the Entrelac Stole, I knit squares made of garter stitch placed on an angle instead, to create a pointed border. This creates a more interesting top and bottom edge and leaves a nice place to attach the tassels. Rather than casting on the total number of stitches for the entire stole, I cast on and knit only the stitches for the first square. I cast on additional stitches from the first square to make the second square, and so on until four squares were completed.

Entrelac does not have straight edges, so you must add edge triangles. The edge triangles of entrelac look similar to those found in interlocking diamonds, but the process for making them is very different. For right-edge triangles, you work increases to make straight edges while at the same time working decreases to join the triangle to the adjacent square. For left-edge triangles, you decrease picked-up stitches at the edge to make the edge straight. It's all rather amazing when you watch it happen as you knit.

MATERIALS

3 skeins of Cool Stuff by Prism (mixed fiber
content, 300yds/8oz); color Periwinkle
Size 8 US (5mm) knitting needles, or size
required to obtain gauge

Gauge: 16 sts and 24 rows = 4"

DIRECTIONS

Beginning squares (shown in pink on diagram)
CO 12 sts, K 24 rows.

Leave the 12 sts just worked on the needle.
Using cable CO, CO 12 sts. K 24 rows using only
the 12 sts just CO. Leave the 24 sts just worked on
the needle. Using cable CO, CO 12 sts. K 24 rows
using only the 12 sts just CO. Leave the 36 sts just
worked on the needle. Using cable CO, CO 12
sts. K 24 rows using only the 12 sts just CO; 48 sts.
This creates 4 beginning squares that slant toward
the right.

****Right side triangle (shown in blue on
diagram)**
Inc in first st. Turn, P2. Turn, inc in first st, SSK
(this will join the right side triangle to beginning
square 4), turn, sl 1, P to end. Turn, inc in first st,
K1, SSK. Turn, sl 1, P to end. Turn, inc in first st,
K2, SSK. Turn, sl 1, P to end. Turn, inc in first st,
K3, SSK. Turn, sl 1, P to end. Turn, inc in first st,
K4, SSK. Turn, sl 1, P to end. Turn, inc in first st,
K5, SSK. Turn, sl 1, P to end. Turn, inc in first st,
K6, SSK. Turn, sl 1, P to end. Turn, inc in first st,
K7, SSK. Turn, sl 1, P to end. Turn, inc in first st,
K8, SSK. Turn, sl 1, P to end. Turn, inc in first st,
K9, SSK; 12 sts on right needle. Turn, sl 1, P to
end. Turn, K11, SSK. All sts of beginning square

4 should be used up. Leave all sts on needle. This
creates triangle 5.

**Left slanting squares (shown in yellow on
diagram)**
Pick up 12 sts kw down left edge of square 4 of
beginning squares. *Turn, sl 1, P to end. Turn,
K11, SSK.* Turn, sl 1, P to end. Repeat from * to
* until all sts of square 3 are used (this creates
square 6). Pick up 12 sts down left edge of square
3. Repeat from * to * until all sts of square 2 are
used (this creates square 7). Pick up 12 sts down
left edge of square 2. Repeat from * to * until all
sts of square 1 are used (this creates square 8).

Left side triangle (shown in green on diagram)
Pick up 12 sts kw down left edge of square 1 of
beginning squares. *Turn, P. Turn, K to 3 sts from
the end, K2tog, K1.* Repeat from * to * until 2 sts
remain.*** This creates triangle 9.

**Right-slanting squares (shown in orange in
diagram)**
Pick up 10 sts pw down right edge of left side triangle just worked. *Turn, sl 1, K to end. Turn, P
11, P2tog* (this creates square 10 and joins it to
square 8). Repeat from * to * until all sts of square
8 are used. Pick up 12 sts pw down right edge of
square 8. Repeat from * to * (this creates square
11). Pick up 12 sts pw down right edge of square
7. Repeat from * to * (this creates square 12). Pick
up 12 sts pw down right edge of square 6. Repeat
from * to * (this creates square 13). ** Repeat from
** to ** 11 more times, then from ** to *** once.

**Ending squares (shown in lavender in
diagram)**
These squares slant toward the right and are
worked in garter stitch.

Pick up 10 sts pw down right edge of left side

triangle just worked.† Turn, sl 1 wyif, K to end. Turn, K11, K2tog.† Repeat from † to † until all sts of square you are joining to are used, turn, sl 1 wyif, K to end. Turn, BO all sts loosely. This makes square 118.†† Pick up 11 sts pw down right edge of square just joined to. Repeat from † to †† 3 times, creating squares 119, 120, and 121. Finish off.

FINISHING

Weave in all ends and gently steam edges. Make 8 tassels using a piece of 5" cardboard and wrapping yarn 20 times. Attach tassels to the points of the beginning and ending squares as indicated on diagram. See "Tassel Basics" on page 11.

INTARSIA

ONE OF THE more beautiful forms of knitting is intarsia. In the dictionary, intarsia is defined as a technique of using inlaid patterns to decorate a surface, especially of wood. Intarsia knitting features "inlays" of new colors of yarn in areas of knitting. The various shapes and motifs that we can knit into our projects make this some of the most beautiful knitting that exists. It is one technique, however, that a lot of knitters avoid because it looks like so much work. Lots of different colors, a huge chart, and lots of ends to weave in when finished often scare people off from the pleasure of "painting" with knitting. There are three important things to consider when you use this technique.

First, intarsia knitting is done flat. It must be worked by knitting a row, turning the work, and purling the return row. The working yarns will be at the wrong end of the work if you try to do this without seams. There are some forms of circular intarsia, but true, by-the-book intarsia is knit back and forth.

Second, what yarns should you use? I don't think there is a yarn that exists that you can't use for intarsia. The real question is "What yarns don't work as well?" Some of the more textured or "hairy" yarns hide little idiosyncrasies that can occur in intarsia knitting, but they might make the finished piece too fuzzy.

Cotton and silk, I think, are among the hardest fibers to work with because "what you knit is what you get." They don't stretch to fill in little problem areas and they tend to be slippery. The ends also need to be woven in a bit more since

they can slip out easily and work their way to the right side.

I really like to work with wool and wool blends for intarsia. They feel good in your hands and are easy to knit. The ends weave in nicely, you can hide problem areas easily, and you can block and steam the knitting to make it behave. The yarn used in your design does not have to be the same brand or fiber content as the yarn listed in the following patterns, but it should knit at the same gauge. Yarn with a slight difference in weight and gauge will work if it is used in small amounts, but be sure all yarns will clean, wash, and block the same.

Third, each section of knitting requires its own ball or strand of yarn. In true intarsia, the yarns do not float across the back of the work. Most intarsia patterns recommend using bobbins to hold each of the yarns at the back of the work in small balls that won't unwind. There are various kinds of bobbins, and you may have to experiment with several to find the one you prefer. Plastic bobbins

Bobbins

come in a couple of sizes; choose a size appropriate for the amount of yarn you need for a section.

One of my favorite ways to make a bobbin of yarn is called the butterfly. It doesn't require a plastic or other commercial bobbin at all; you wind the yarn on your fingers to resemble butterfly wings. The butterfly isn't heavy and can actually get quite large. It will eventually fall apart, but at that point you will have used enough of the yarn that you can just let it hang off the knitting or rewind it. The other option is to use a strand of yarn not wound on a bobbin or into a butterfly and let it hang straight off the back of the knitting.

Steps for winding a butterfly:

1. Place end of yarn across your left hand and wind yarn around thumb and small finger.

2. Continue to bring yarn around your small finger and back across hand and around your thumb again. Continue with this motion to make a figure eight with the yarn.

3. When you have wound as much yarn as you need, break off yarn from the ball and wind around center of the butterfly. Tuck in the end.

4. Remove butterfly from your hand.

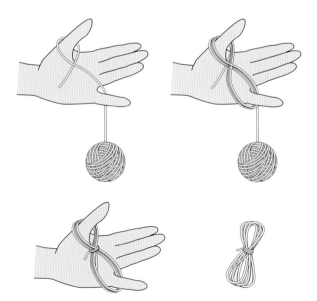

Guidelines for using the various types of bobbins:

- 1 to 20 stitches in a motif: Use a strand of yarn with no bobbin.

- 21 to 100 stitches in a motif: Use a small bobbin or butterfly.

- 101 or more stitches in a motif: Use a large bobbin or butterfly.

A rough estimate for yarn usage is about one inch of yarn per stitch. This will, of course, vary slightly depending on the weight of the yarn.

PREPARING CHARTS

You can design your own charts for knitting intarsia. It's a wonderful process, but just in case you don't want to design your own, there are plenty of intarsia patterns available commercially. To design your own charts, you must draw whatever you are going to knit—the motifs, squares, houses, trees, or whatever—at the same gauge you will use when you knit. If your knitting gauge is five stitches and seven rows for one inch, then the graph paper you use has to be the same gauge. If you use graph paper with four squares per inch, the shape you draw will not be the shape you knit. Knit stitches are not square; they are wider than they are tall, so you can't use square graph paper to draw your pattern. Use knitter's graph paper instead.

To use the graph paper, tape or paste together enough sheets to equal the largest section of the garment. Draw in the shaping for the armholes, neck, and any side shaping that you might need. Now you can begin to draw in your color work. When you have the whole piece in front of you, it is easy to see where the pictures you draw will end

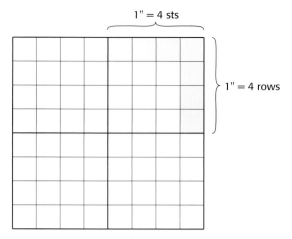

1" = 4 sts

1" = 4 rows

Regular Graph Paper

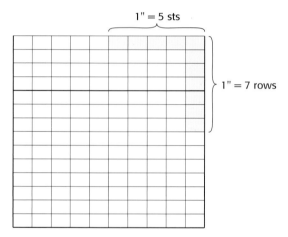

1" = 5 sts

1" = 7 rows

Knitter's Graph Paper

up on the finished piece. This will eliminate surprises later. Even if you use a computer program to design your sweater chart, taking the time to sketch the design in advance will save you time spent moving things around on the computer screen, printing, moving again, and so on.

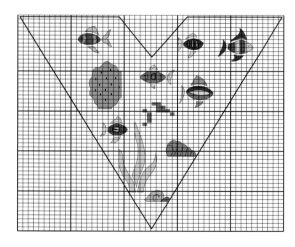

Although it is a good idea to sketch the design in advance, it is actually fun to fill in the colors and change things around on the computer. I spent days and days on the chart for the Autumn Leaves Shawl, changing colors around, moving the leaves, charting the border. While I was knitting the project, then, I was able to make changes if I felt something wasn't quite right and then update the chart on the computer.

GETTING STARTED

I like to knit intarsia while sitting at a table. I can keep the chart flat, my ruler in place, and all of my yarns and accessories handy. Using colored pencils, color in the motifs on your chart so you don't have to read the color symbols, which can sometimes look alike and be confusing. Often, I will prewind bobbins in anticipation of what is going to happen next in the chart. I don't like to have to stop and wind a bobbin in the middle of a row.

Mark off the rows with a pencil as you complete them, and keep your place with a ruler or stick-on note as described on page 7. If the chart is large, it is helpful to mark off the middle of the row as well. Actually, marking along the edge of the motif being knit is helpful too.

Starting a new yarn seems to leave the largest hole in an intarsia pattern. This bothers a lot of people as they are knitting, even though the hole will get closed when the end is woven in. There is a terrific method for starting a new strand of yarn developed by Sherry Stuever and Keely Stuever from Sealed With A Kiss, Inc. These two ladies have created and knit more intarsia patterns than anyone else I know. Their method for starting a new strand is as follows:

When you come to a place where you want to introduce a new color, lay the tail of the new yarn between the knitting needles and toward the front of the work. Keep the new bobbin toward the back of the work. Now move the yarn you are dropping to the left over the top of the new yarn. The new color will then come toward the right from underneath as it does in the normal "twist" used when changing colors. This will lock the new color in place. The tail that is now on the front of the work will be pushed through the knitting to the back of the work when the end gets woven in. You can also use this technique whenever you start a new ball of yarn in the middle of the row in any knitting project.

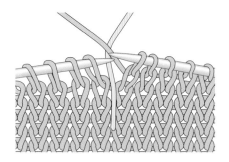

You must also do a "twist" every time you change a color. This twist or interlock is the same regardless of where you are in the knitting. If you always follow the steps below, you will never have holes in the knitting from changing colors.

Take the color you are dropping and move it to the left, leaving it on top. Pick up the new color from underneath and pull it to the right and begin knitting or purling with it. All twists should occur on the wrong side of the work. You will know you have twisted correctly if, after a few rows, you can see the colors intertwined or braided where they change on the wrong side—and, of course, if there are no holes.

For continental knitters the steps are the same except for a few small differences. The yarn you are dropping is already in the left hand and located on top. So leave it there, pick up the new

color with the right hand, which moves it to the right from underneath, and place it in the left hand. Continental knitters have the benefit of leaving out the part about moving the yarn to the left hand, but they have to add moving the new color to the left hand.

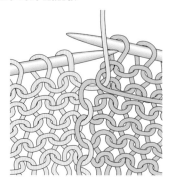

Wrong side of work.
Interwoven colors show correct twist on interlock.

There are times where it will look like you don't need to go through the steps to make the yarns interlock, for example, when the color work is producing a diagonal line. But if you *always* go through the above steps to make the twist or interlock, you will always be successful with intarsia knitting. You won't have holes and the yarns will always be twisted correctly on the back.

Intarsia knitting always requires steaming or blocking to look perfect. Don't fret if the knitting looks uneven or lumpy. When all the ends are woven in and the piece has been blocked it will look one hundred percent better.

The two projects included in this chapter look very different from each other, but both utilize intarsia at its best. The Smoke Intarsia Scarf is a good way to learn the technique, and the Autumn Leaves Shawl is a great way to show off your expertise.

Smoke Intarsia Scarf

MATERIALS

- Color A: 2 skeins of Soft by Prism (100% nylon, 88yds/50g); color Smoke
- Color B: 2 skeins of Andee by Prism (50% alpaca, 50% wool, 144yds/50g); color Smoke
- Size 8 US (5mm) knitting needles, or size required to obtain gauge

- Gauge: 18 stitches and 26 rows = 4" using Andee in stockinette stitch

DIRECTIONS

NOTE: *All rows are charted.*

CO 6 sts using color A and begin chart. Work rows 1 through 36. Repeat rows "a" and "b" until work measures approximately 59" from the beginning. Work rows 37 through 71. BO.

FINISHING

Gently steam to flatten scarf where yarns and pattern stitch change.

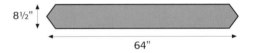

8½"

64"

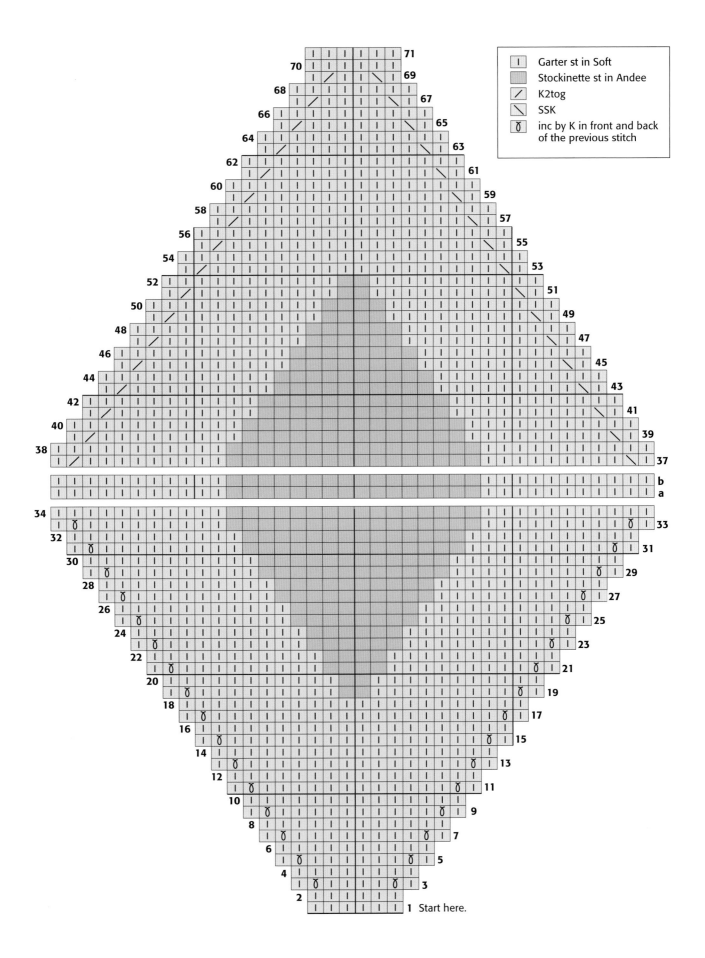

Garter st in Soft
Stockinette st in Andee
K2tog
SSK
inc by K in front and back of the previous stitch

1 Start here.

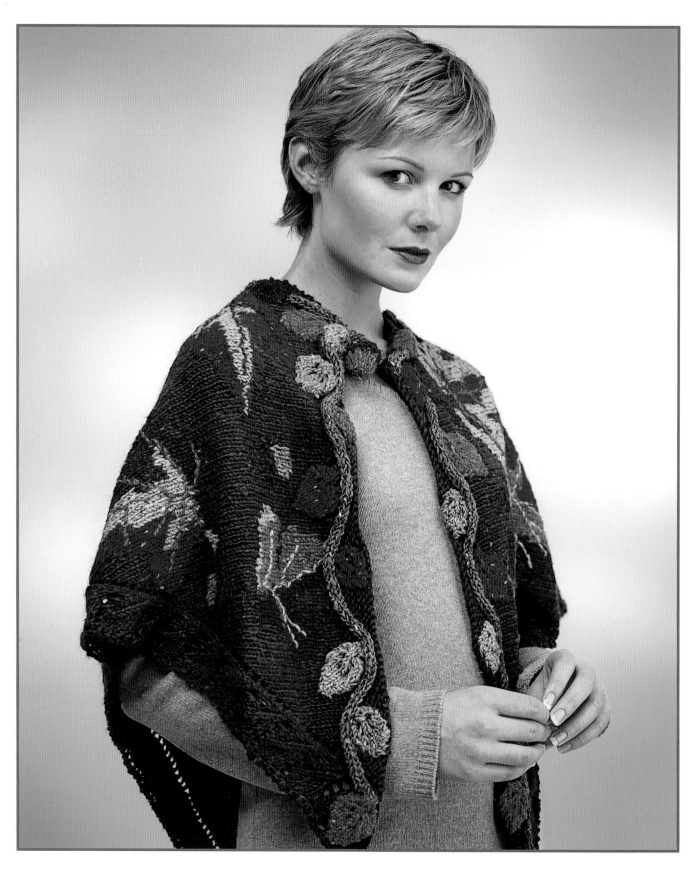

MATERIALS

Tahki Donegal Tweed (100% wool,
   183yds/100g) in the following amounts:
   4 skeins color 0878 (Main Color)
   1 skein each of the following colors:
      0845 Purple
      0840 Red
      0802 Gold
      0891 Rust
      0879 Leaf Green
      0803 Grass Green
      0864 Dark Rust
      0893 Orange
      0801 Beige
Size 9 US (5.5mm) knitting needles, or size
   required to obtain gauge
Two size 8 US (5mm) double-pointed needles
   for leaves and I cord

Gauge: 16 sts and 24 rows = 4" in stockinette
   stitch

DIRECTIONS

NOTE: *All rows are charted.*

Using size 9 needle and color 0878, CO 3 sts
and begin chart as shown. When each side is completed, bind off loosely.

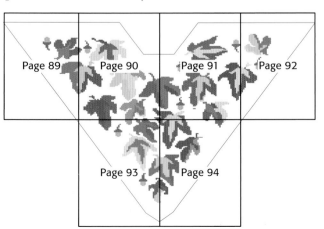

LEAVES FOR EMBELLISHMENT

With size 8 dpn and color 0801, work 2 yards of
3-stitch I cord (see page 8). Following diagram on
page 88, tack down I cord to edge of shawl, making button loop at right neck.

With size 8 dpn, CO 3 sts. Begin chart. K13
leaves in colors indicated.

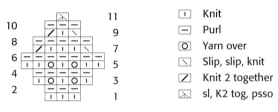

Color	Number of Leaves
0845	1
0840	3
0802	2
0803	3
0864	1
0893	3

Using size 8 dpn, CO 3 sts. Begin chart. Knit
12 leaves in colors indicated.

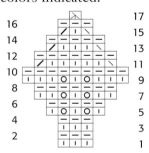

Color	Number of Leaves
0802	3
0891	2
0803	2
0864	2
0893	3

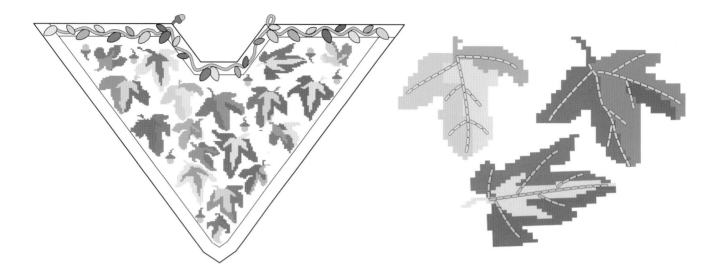

Sew leaves to shawl using drawing above for placement.

Acorn closure

Using size 8 dpn and color 0801, CO 5 sts.

Row 1 (RS): Inc in each st; 10 sts.

Row 2, 4, 6, and 8: P.

Row 3, 5, and 7: K.

Change to color 0864.

Row 1: K1 (inc in next 8 sts) K1; 18 sts.

Row 2, 3, 4, 5, 6: K.

Row 7: K2tog across; 9 sts.

Row 8: K1, (K2tog) 4 times; 5 sts.

Row 9: K2tog twice, K1; 3 sts.

Working on 3 sts, K 2" of I cord. BO. Using scraps of color 0801, stuff the acorn and sew the seam closed. Attach I cord to left front. Tuck the end of the I cord under a leaf.

FINISHING

Weave in all ends and steam gently. Use a running stitch to embroider veins on the leaves, using colors shown in drawing.

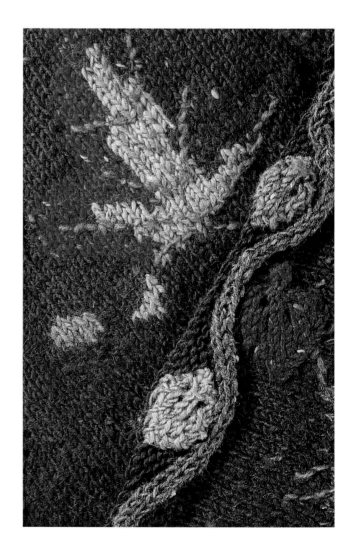

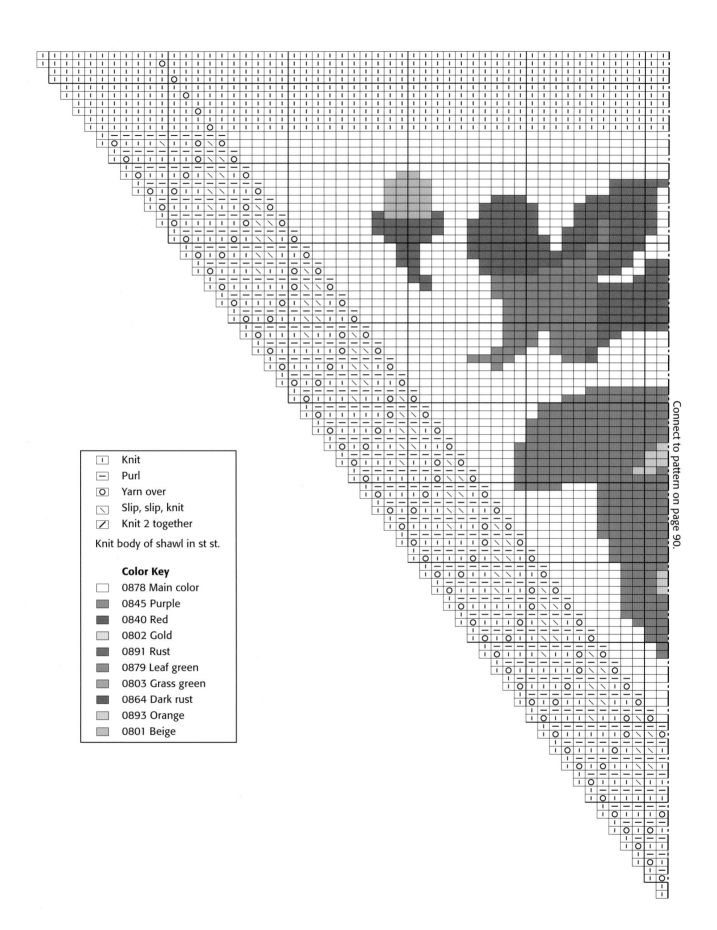

Knit

Purl

Yarn over

Slip, slip, knit

Knit 2 together

Knit body of shawl in st st.

Color Key

0878 Main color

0845 Purple

0840 Red

0802 Gold

0891 Rust

0879 Leaf green

0803 Grass green

0864 Dark rust

0893 Orange

0801 Beige

Connect to pattern on page 90.

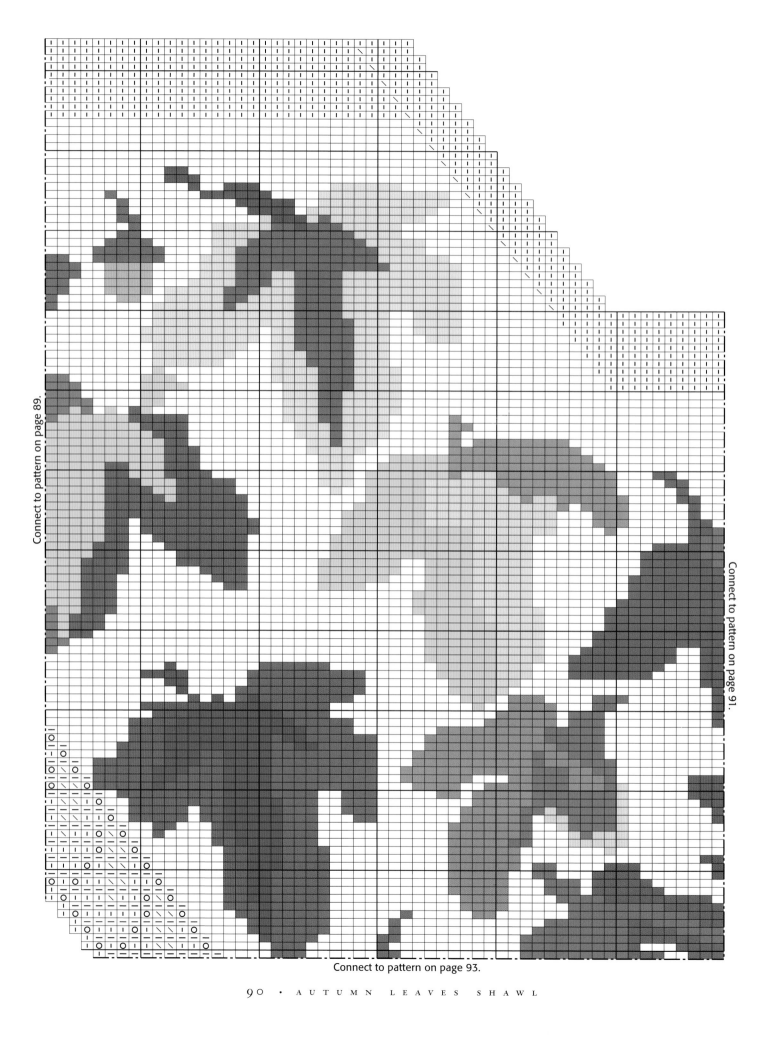

Connect to pattern on page 89.

Connect to pattern on page 91.

Connect to pattern on page 93.

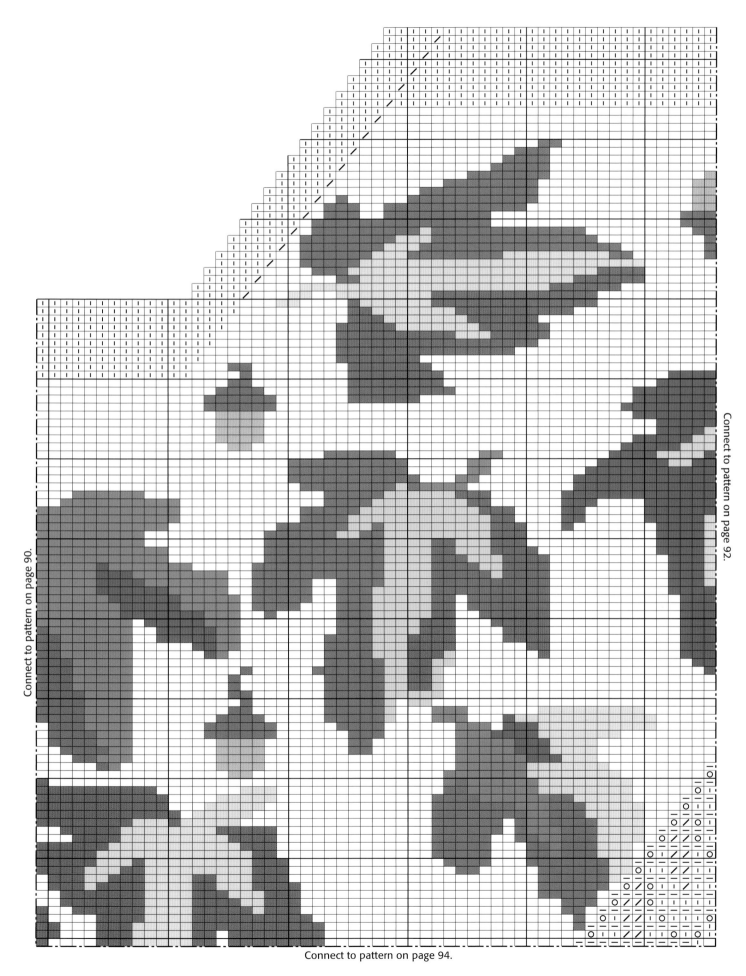

Connect to pattern on page 90.

Connect to pattern on page 92.

Connect to pattern on page 94.

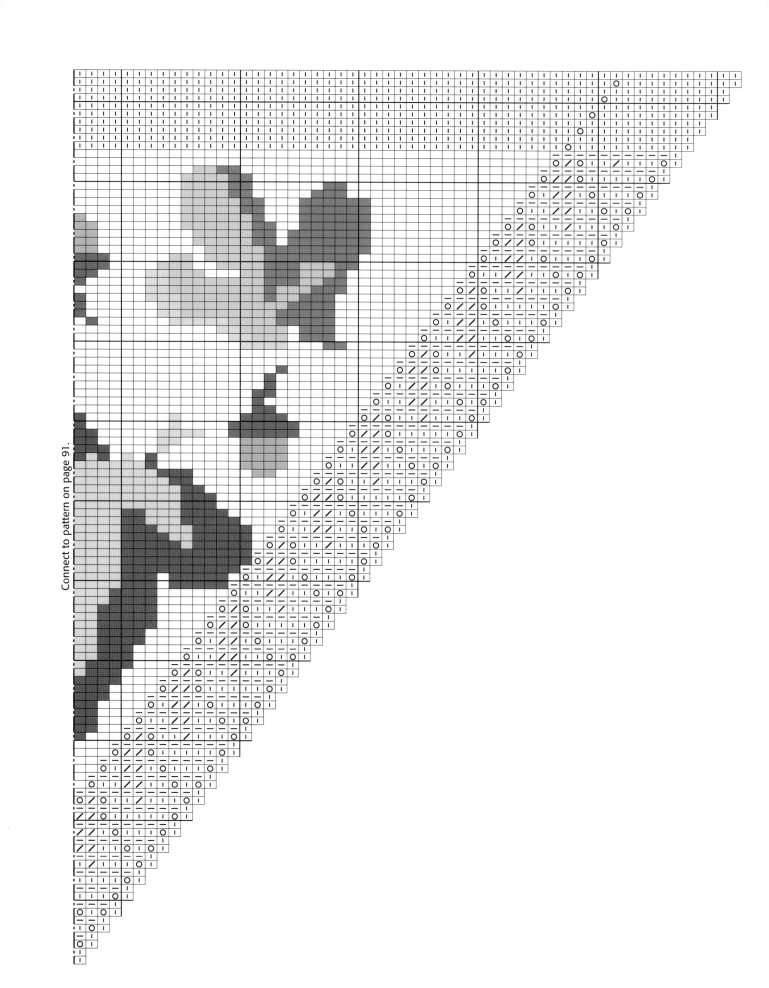

Connect to pattern on page 91.

Connect to pattern on page 90.

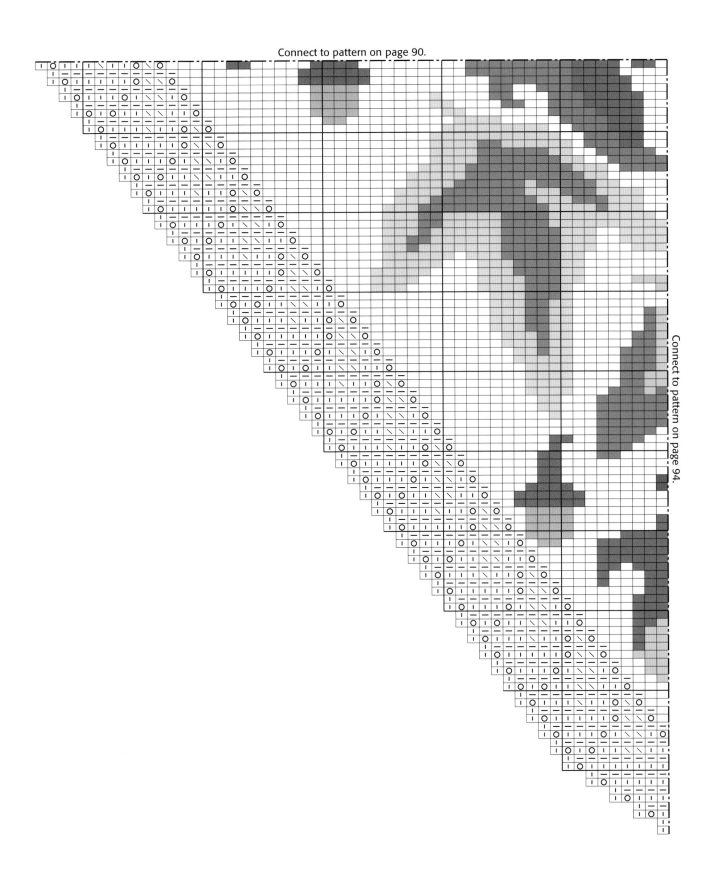

Connect to pattern on page 94.

Connect to pattern on page 92.

Connect to pattern on page 93.

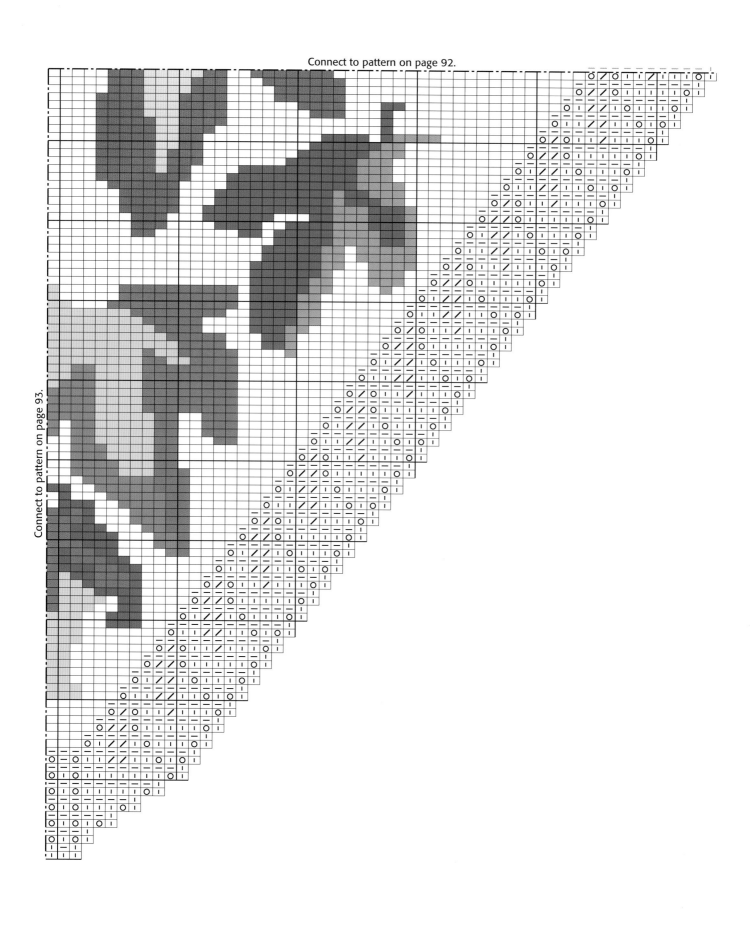

BIBLIOGRAPHY

Epstein, Nicky. *Nicky Epstein's Knitted Embellishments: 350 Appliques, Borders, Cards and More!* Loveland, Colo.: Interweave Press, 1999.

Macdonald, Anne L. *No Idle Hands: the Social History of American Knitting.* New York: Ballantine Books, 1988.

Rutt, Richard. *A History of Hand Knitting.* Loveland, Colo.: Interweave Press, 1987.

Stuever, Sherry and Keely Stuever. *Intarsia: A Workshop for Hand & Machine Knitting.* Guthrie, Okla.: Sealed With A Kiss, Inc., 1998.

Walker, Barbara G. *A Treasury of Knitting Patterns.* Pittsville, Wisc.: Schoolhouse Press, 1998.

———. *A Second Treasury of Knitting Patterns.* Pittsville, Wisc.: Schoolhouse Press, 1998.

———. *Charted Knitting Designs: A Third Treasury of Knitting Patterns.* New York: Macmillan, 1972.

Wiseman, Nancie. *Lace from the Attic: A Victorian Notebook of Knitted Lace Patterns.* Loveland, Colo.: Interweave Press, 1998.

RESOURCES

BERROCO, INC.
Uxbridge, Mass.
(800) 343-4948
yarn (wholesale only)

CRYSTAL PALACE YARNS
Berkeley, Calif.
www.straw.com/cpy
(800) 666-7455
yarn and needles (wholesale and retail)

THE GREAT ADIRONDACK YARN CO.
Amsterdam, N.Y.
(518) 843-3381
yarn (wholesale only)

KNIT ONE, CROCHET TOO
Ventura, Calif.
(800) 607-2462
e-mail: K1C2@ix.netcom.com
yarn (wholesale only)

LOUET SALES
Ogdensburg, N.Y.
www.louet.com
yarn (wholesale and retail)

MOUNTAIN COLORS YARN
Corvallis, Mont.
(406) 777-3377
e-mail: redfox@bitterroot.net
yarn (wholesale only)

MUENCH YARNS & BUTTONS
Novato, Calif.
e-mail: muenchyarn@aol.com
(800) 733-9276
yarn and needles (wholesale only)

PRISM YARNS
St. Petersburg, Fla.
(727) 327-3100
yarn (wholesale only)

SEALED WITH A KISS, INC.
Guthrie, Okla.
(405) 282-8649
Intarsia patterns and kits

TAHKI IMPORTS LTD.
Moonachie, N.J.
(800) 338-YARN (9276)
www.tahki.com
yarn (wholesale only)

TRENDSETTER YARNS
Van Nuys, Calif.
e-mail: trndstr@aol.com
(800) 446-2425
(818) 780-5497
yarn (wholesale only)

UNIQUE KOLOURS, LTD.
Downingtown, Pa.
(800) 252-DYE4
e-mail: uniquekolo@aol.com
yarn, including colinette yarns (wholesale only)

new and bestselling titles from

America's Best-Loved Craft & Hobby Books®

America's Best-Loved Quilt Books®

NEW RELEASES
1000 Great Quilt Blocks
Basically Brilliant Knits
Bright Quilts from Down Under
Christmas Delights
Creative Machine Stitching
Crochet for Tots
Crocheted Aran Sweaters
Cutting Corners
Everyday Embellishments
Folk Art Friends
Garden Party
Hocus Pocus!
Just Can't Cut It!
Quilter's Home: Winter, The
Sweet and Simple Baby Quilts
Time to Quilt
Today's Crochet
Traditional Quilts to Paper Piece

APPLIQUÉ
Appliquilt in the Cabin
Artful Album Quilts
Artful Appliqué
Blossoms in Winter
Color-Blend Appliqué
Sunbonnet Sue All through the Year

BABY QUILTS
Easy Paper-Pieced Baby Quilts
Even More Quilts for Baby
More Quilts for Baby
Play Quilts
Quilted Nursery, The
Quilts for Baby

HOLIDAY QUILTS & CRAFTS
Christmas Cats and Dogs
Creepy Crafty Halloween
Handcrafted Christmas, A
Make Room for Christmas Quilts
Welcome to the North Pole

HOME DECORATING
Decorated Kitchen, The
Decorated Porch, The
Dresden Fan
Gracing the Table
Make Room for Quilts
Quilts for Mantels and More
Sweet Dreams

LEARNING TO QUILT
101 Fabulous Rotary-Cut Quilts
Beyond the Blocks
Casual Quilter, The
Feathers That Fly
Joy of Quilting, The
Simple Joys of Quilting, The
Your First Quilt Book (or it should be!)

PAPER PIECING
40 Bright and Bold Paper-Pieced Blocks
50 Fabulous Paper-Pieced Stars
For the Birds
Quilter's Ark, A
Rich Traditions
Split-Diamond Dazzlers

ROTARY CUTTING
365 Quilt Blocks a Year Perpetual Calendar
Around the Block Again
Around the Block with Judy Hopkins
Fat Quarter Quilts
More Fat Quarter Quilts
Stack the Deck!
Triangle Tricks
Triangle-Free Quilts

SCRAP QUILTS
Nickel Quilts
Scrap Frenzy
Scrappy Duos
Spectacular Scraps
Strips and Strings
Successful Scrap Quilts

TOPICS IN QUILTMAKING
American Stenciled Quilts
Americana Quilts
Batik Beauties
Bed and Breakfast Quilts
Fabulous Quilts from Favorite Patterns
Frayed-Edge Fun
Patriotic Little Quilts
Reversible Quilts

CRAFTS
ABCs of Making Teddy Bears, The
Blissful Bath, The
Handcrafted Frames
Handcrafted Garden Accents
Handprint Quilts
Painted Chairs
Painted Whimsies

KNITTING & CROCHET
365 Knitting Stitches a Year Perpetual Calendar
Clever Knits
Crochet for Babies and Toddlers
Crocheted Sweaters
Knitted Sweaters for Every Season
Knitted Throws and More
Knitter's Book of Finishing Techniques, The
Knitter's Template, A
More Paintbox Knits
Paintbox Knits
Too Cute! Cotton Knits for Toddlers
Treasury of Rowan Knits, A
Ultimate Knitter's Guide, The

Our books are available at bookstores and your favorite craft, fabric, and yarn retailers. If you don't see the title you're looking for, visit us at **www.martingale-pub.com** or contact us at:

1-800-426-3126

International: 1-425-483-3313

Fax: 1-425-486-7596

Email: info@martingale-pub.com

For more information and a full list of our titles, visit our Web site.